The Merchant of Venice

Graham Holderness was born in ⟨...⟩
College, Oxford. His academ⟨...⟩ ⟨...⟩arch
work at the Open Univers⟨...⟩ ⟨...⟩n at the
University College of Swa⟨...⟩ Literature
and Drama at Swansea Univ⟨...⟩ ⟨...⟩dult Education
(1982–7), Headship of the Depa⟨...⟩ Roehampton Insti-
tute (1987–91) and the Professorshi⟨...⟩ ⟨...⟩s at Hatfield Polytech-
nic (1991–2). He is currently Profe⟨...⟩ Dean of the School of
Humanities and Education at the Unive⟨...⟩y of Hertfordshire.

His publications include *D. H. Lawrence: History, Ideology and Fiction* (1982), *Shakespeare's History* (1985), *Wuthering Heights* (1985), *Women in Love* (1986), *Hamlet* (1987), *The Taming of the Shrew* (1989) and the Penguin Critical Studies of *Richard II* (1989) and *Romeo and Juliet* (1991). He has also edited *The Shakespeare Myth* (1988), *The Politics of Theatre and Drama* (1992) and *Shakespeare's History Plays: Richard II to Henry V* (1992). He is currently working with Bryan Loughrey on a new edition of Shakespeare's plays based on the original printed texts and is co-author of *Shakespeare: The Play of History* (1988) and *Shakespeare: Out of Court* (1990)

Penguin Critical Studies
Advisory Editor: Bryan Loughrey

William Shakespeare

The Merchant of Venice

Graham Holderness

Penguin Books

PENGUIN BOOKS

Published by the Penguin Group
Penguin Books Ltd, 27 Wrights Lane, London W8 5TZ, England
Penguin Books USA Inc., 375 Hudson Street, New York, New York 10014, USA
Penguin Books Australia Ltd, Ringwood, Victoria, Australia
Penguin Books Canada Ltd, 10 Alcorn Avenue, Toronto, Ontario, Canada M4V 3B2
Penguin Books (NZ) Ltd, 182–190 Wairau Road, Auckland 10, New Zealand

Penguin Books Ltd, Registered Offices: Harmondsworth, Middlesex, England

First published 1993
10 9 8 7 6 5 4 3 2

Typeset by Datix International Limited, Bungay, Suffolk
Filmset in 9/11pt Monophoto Times
Printed in England by Clays Ltd, St Ives plc

Contents

Introduction

The Merchant of Venice was clearly understood, when it was originally produced and published, to be a comedy. It appears, under the simple title *The Merchant of Venice*, grouped under the heading 'Comedies' in the first collected edition of Shakespeare's works, the First Folio of 1623. But, to many subsequent readers, critics, actors, directors and playgoers, *The Merchant of Venice* has seemed much more difficult to define straightforwardly in comic terms; on the contrary, it often seems to have read and played more like a 'problem play', or even a tragedy.

No other Shakespeare comedy before *All's Well that Ends Well* (1602) and *Measure for Measure* (1604), perhaps no other Shakespeare comedy at all, has excited comparable controversy (Walter Cohen, 1982).[1]

The Merchant of Venice is, among other things, as much a 'problem' play as one by Ibsen or Shaw (W. H. Auden, 1963).[2]

Indeed, seen from any angle, *The Merchant of Venice* is not a very funny play, and we might gain a lot if, for the moment, we ceased to be bullied by its inclusion in the comedies (Graham Midgely, 1960).[3]

I must include *The Merchant of Venice* among the tragedies, although the frame of the work is a composition of laughing masks and sunny faces . . . as though the poet *meant* to write a comedy (Heinrich Heine, 1839).[4]

We have to be careful in our assumptions about what comedy meant to the Elizabethans. Dramatic comedies needn't necessarily, for example, have been particularly funny, though they were likely to contain substantial ingredients of wit and humour. And although modern criticism has largely accepted the other generic definitions proposed by the First Folio – tragedy and history – it is precisely within the category of comedy that problems of theoretical definition have been encountered – even to the point where some plays (*Measure for Measure*, *All's Well That Ends Well*, *Troilus and Cressida*) have been disentangled from the comedies group by modern critics and redefined as 'problem plays'.[5] *The Merchant of Venice* has, as W. H. Auden suggested, a lot in common with those generically problematical plays. Perhaps in the sixteenth century the concept of comedy was broader and more elastic than it is today, containing all that we think of as comic, but also incorporating much that we would regard as rather more serious.

vii

Comedy or Tragedy?

Rough working definitions of genre can, however, be made by comparing the Folio's three categories: comedy, tragedy and history. *The Merchant of Venice* is not a tragedy, we can say with some confidence, because its central character, Antonio (the merchant of the title), is ultimately saved from disaster and death – unlike the hero of Shakespeare's other Venetian drama, *Othello*, which is definitely by all accounts accepted as a tragedy. It is not a history play (although the earliest printed text, the First Quarto of 1600, from which all other texts of the play derive, described it as a 'comicall History'), since its plot is drawn from fictional romance and folk-tale stories rather than from historiographical narratives.

The main thematic and structural elements of the play all seem to belong within the category of romantic comedy rather than elsewhere. The basic action of the play is mobilized by the intertwining of two stories: Bassanio's courtship of the wealthy heiress, Portia of Belmont, which is straightforward romance; and the story of the 'flesh-bond', which was a narrative type of some antiquity, though probably known to Shakespeare through an Italian romance written in the late fourteenth century.[6] What ties the plots together is the friendship or love of Antonio and Bassanio, which becomes the background for a story of hatred and revenge. Bassanio's need for money to support the expenses of his courtship induces him to borrow from Antonio, who in turn has to apply for a loan from the Jewish moneylender, or usurer, Shylock. A member of a racial and religious minority within the predominantly Christian society of Venice, Shylock hates Christians in general, and Antonio in particular, for their racial and economic hostility towards him and his business of moneylending (the 'Christians' do not actually see themselves as Christians, but rather as a normative social group – it is only from the alienated perspective of Judaism that they are regarded as 'Christians'). Seeing an opportunity to gain advantage over Antonio, Shylock proposes the flesh-bond, by means of which Antonio agrees, if the debt is not settled within the agreed term, to permit Shylock to cut off a pound of his flesh. Side by side with the playful glamour of romance we find the implacable enmity and vindictiveness characteristic of revenge tragedy. Counterpoised to the elegant fiction of the three caskets, with its overtones of fairy-tale and magic, appears the grotesque violence of the flesh-bond – a moral or financial debt payable by physical mutilation – which again would not be out of place in a Senecan melodrama like *Titus Andronicus*, or in a Jacobean revenge tragedy.

The courtship plot combines the sophisticated wittiness and verbal playfulness of courtly comedy with the simple emotions and narrative typologies of romance, exemplified in the motif of the three caskets: by the terms of her father's will, Portia is not free to choose her own marriage partner, but must accept the suitor who chooses correctly from the three caskets. Two suitors – the Princes of Morocco and Arragon – choose wrongly and, in the event, the ritual of choice delivers the suitor she herself prefers – Bassanio. The courtship romance operates as smoothly and predictably as a fairy-tale. Two contenders choose wrongly, and success falls to the third: an apparently arbitrary ritual, seemingly based on chance, succeeds perfectly in acquiring the suitor Portia wants, and ridding her of various unwanted applicants for her hand and fortune. In the commercial world of Venice, however (so different, at least at face value, from the fairy-tale world of Belmont), reliance on luck does not necessarily produce such gratifying results. Immediately after this resolution of the romance plot, news is delivered that Antonio's ships have been lost, and that he is unable to repay Shylock's loan. The bond is forfeit, and Shylock is legally entitled to take his forfeit from Antonio's body.

Thus the romance narrative precipitates, through the realistic factor of Bassanio's need to borrow money to sustain a gentlemanly lifestyle, Antonio's entering into the dangerous bond with Shylock, which entails his exposure to life-threatening perils. Bassanio's supportive friendship, even when augmented by Portia's wealth, proves powerless to help. The Duke of Venice has to uphold Shylock's right to proceed with his deadly suit against Antonio, since in terms of Venetian law, the moneylender has an unanswerable case. But in winning Portia, Bassanio has not only gained happiness and wealth, he has also acquired the services of someone far more resourceful, enterprising and intelligent than either himself or any of his Venetian companions. Portia quickly disguises herself as a lawyer and defends Antonio's case with masterful legal skill, producing other statutes which not only prevent Shylock from proceeding, but also turn the judicial tables and render Shylock vulnerable to the death penalty for conspiring against Antonio's life. Once Shylock is defeated, the Christian community is prepared to offer him what they regard as a merciful settlement: his life is spared, on condition that he become converted to Christianity, and that half his wealth is handed over to Antonio, who will keep it in trust for the benefit of Shylock's runaway daughter, Jessica.

The minor plot involving the abduction of Jessica, Shylock's daughter, by Lorenzo, belongs to another, rather harsher type of comedy –

the 'Italian comedy' – which formed the basis for the popular English 'city comedy' of the seventeenth century. This dramatic form, which typically pitted the poor but romantic young against the rich and tyrannical old, consisted of conventional plots and stock characters – the resourceful young hero, the beautiful young heroine, the avaricious father, the scheming servant. Within this generic context, Shylock becomes the miser who serves as an object of ridicule and abuse, while the youthful hero and heroine swindle and desert him, to the unprincipled but unproblematical pleasure of the audience. The whole of the play's last act abandons the dangerously contemporary world of Venice for the fairy-tale retreat of Belmont, and provides the spectator with an unadulterated diet of comic and romantic narrative pleasures – courtly wit-contests, lists of great lovers, romantic reconciliations, clarified misunderstandings, cast-off disguises, music and marriage.

Yet all these characteristics and distinctions of comedy have raised problems for modern criticism of the play. *The Merchant of Venice* is a comedy of ultimate success for Antonio, but a tragic narrative of suffering and loss for Shylock. The story of the flesh-bond was to be found in fiction rather than history, but Shakespeare transposed it to a real historical place – Venice – which represented for sixteenth-century Europeans a highly advanced type of social organization, with very modern economic and political systems. The Venice of Shakespeare's romantic comedy *The Merchant* must paradoxically have seemed a more accurate representation of a real modern world than the fourteenth and fifteenth-century England of his historical dramas. That teasing interplay of the real and the imaginary, exemplified in the relationship between Venice and Belmont, produces a particularly difficult crux for the modern reader in relation to the figure of Shylock. For Shylock is not simply a stock figure of Italian comedy, or the abstracted persecutor of a timeless folk-tale: he is a Jewish moneylender, historically located into precisely the kind of commercial economy where such people would have been encountered, in Venice or England. It has often seemed to modern readers of the play that it was able to take for granted an attitude towards Jews which would necessarily appear in the modern context as unacceptably racist, or even Fascist in character. When Shylock is placed into a city comedy narrative in which his daughter robs and abandons him to marry a Christian, our responses to the conventions of the genre – which should prescribe simple gratification at the success of the lovers, and mocking delight at the discomfiture of the repressive and miserly father – are destabilized by our acute awareness of the complicating factor of race – which discloses the unpleasant awareness that a dominant, majority culture is seen conspiring to rob and humiliate the representative of a minority ethnic group.

The different moral systems governing Venice and Belmont have often been interpreted in the light of ethical oppositions between Law and Love, Justice and Mercy. But as we watch the dominant Christian community which has been threatened collect its powers and concentrate them into a devastating responsive attack on the member of a minority group, it is distinctly possible for the modern reader's pleasures in comedy to be subverted by a deeper sense of racial and political injustice. It has been suggested that the last act of the play needed to focus so exclusively on the alternative world of Belmont in order to obscure these potential suggestions of injustice: to drown in soft music the harsh discords of the trial scene, to rinse from the spectator's mouth with a draught of romantic sweetness the bitter taste of Shylock's humiliation and defeat.

Text and History

There is no direct evidence to indicate how *The Merchant of Venice* was performed on the Elizabethan stage, or perceived by Elizabethan audiences. It may well be, however, that some of its characteristics appeared to resist an easy assimilation into a simple notion of comedy. The descriptive title which appeared in the first printed edition (1600) called it a 'history', and significantly drew attention to features of the play which seem to us in retrospect particularly problematical:

The most excellent
Historie of the *Merchant*
of Venice.
With the extreame crueltie of *Shylocke* the Iewe
towards the sayd Merchant, in cutting a iust pound
of his flesh: and the obtayning of *Portia*
by the choyse of three
chests.
As it hath been divers times acted by the Lord
Chamberlaine his Servants.
Written by William Shakespeare

'Historie' here means something closer to our term 'story' than to historiography and since the genre of the history play (very much a new form in the late sixteenth century) was more sharply defined than either tragedy or comedy, 'history' here cannot mean what it meant when applied to *Richard II* or *Henry V*. But it is at least possible that the inclusion here of 'history', meaning a story of a representative or exemplary kind, was used as an indication that the play was not entirely a fictional romance; that it contained disturbing, perhaps even potentially tragic, elements; and that it was designed to be read as in some way 'true' – implying, that is, some form of mimetic relationship between its narrative and the historical conditions of sixteenth-century Europe, or even England. In *The Taming of the Shrew*, a play which has begun fairly recently to appear highly problematical, comedy is defined as 'a kind of history' and the second edition of *The Merchant* substituted 'comical history' for 'historie'.

The title is then extended into what we would now call a 'blurb', a descriptive blend of information and advertising copy. Within it the publisher neatly calls attention to some of those features of the play that happen to have caused modern readers and audiences most problems. The 'extreame crueltie' of Shylock, with its overtones of revenge drama and its potentiality for a tragic outcome, has often seemed an excessively disturbing action for a comedy. The flesh-bond drama is after all a very close-run thing; it would have needed only a message to miscarry, as in *Romeo and Juliet*, for the plot to resolve itself into a near-comedy rather than a near-tragedy. More importantly, the casting of a Jew ('the Iewe') in the role of revenge villain raises the racial problems suggested earlier: as we shall see, the labelling and addressing of Shylock as 'the Jew', and 'Jew', can prove most disconcerting to modern readings. The reference to the bond and the trial ('a iust pound') focuses on all those difficult questions about law and justice that have dominated subsequent critical interpretation of the play. The allusion to Portia's marriage lottery via the fairy-tale motif of the three chests focuses on the problems raised by the play's generic diversity and by the interpenetration of realist and fictional elements within the drama: why do the reassuring guarantees of romance operate so smoothly for Christians, while the Jew's share of the narrative spoils is loss, humiliation, defeat?

There are two ways of looking at this problem. One is to suggest that in *The Merchant of Venice* we have a work which is essentially historical, in the sense of being strictly confined within the ideological framework, the belief systems and the prejudices of the age in which it was produced; and that the qualities of difficulty, ambivalence and internal conflict discovered in the text by modern criticism are symptomatic not of the character of the play itself, but only of the extent to which certain attitudes have changed. Thus, if it is assumed that the play embodies, from a modern point of view, an extraordinarily casual view of anti-Semitism, that is explained by the prevalence of anti-Semitic prejudices in its surrounding historical context Modern interpreters can in turn adopt two different approaches towards this historicist reading: that the proper responsibility of critical interpretation is to reproduce an appropriate context for the expression of that strictly limited, historically circumscribed character – in short, to read the play as if we were Elizabethans; or that criticism should acknowledge the deep divergences between the ideologies of the past and the culture of the present, and read the play as a document of its time. Differences of interpretation would then arise not from any inherent complexity of the dramatic text, but from the subsequent evolution of cultural differences. Dramatists, readers and playgoers of the 1590s may have shared a basic, unreflective anti-Semitism, but a reader of the later twentieth century, whose views are inevitably coloured by the horrors of the Holocaust, would find it impossible to overlook such a presence within the text of an ideology that has proved in very recent history the source of immense cruelty and suffering.

In that type of reading the ideology of the text is regarded as basically simple, historically conditioned and firmly located in the past. All the complexity, contradiction and ambivalence of modern criticism are produced in retrospective accounts by the facts of historical change. In this school of criticism, which could be called a traditional historicist approach, we should attempt imaginatively to re-enter that past ideology, in order fully to appreciate the drama of that lost culture. In another, typical of certain kinds of post-structuralist criticism such as New Historicism,[7] our responsibility as readers is quite the opposite: we should recognize the past as an enemy, and mobilize our own critical methods in order to confront those questions and problems which we consider to be of paramount importance, although – perhaps even because – writers of the past chose to ignore or minimize their significance. In a traditional historicist reading, we should paradoxically forget the historical specificity of Shylock's racial hatred, and acknowledge his villainy as universal, since the Jewish dimension of the Elizabethan play was only a convenient costume for dramatizing larger ethical concerns about friendship and enmity, justice and mercy. In a New Historicist interpretation, the crudity and prejudice of the play need to be highlighted and exposed by a critical method attuned more closely to the concerns of contemporary theory than to the detail of a vanished history. If the play was anti-Semitic, then that should be recognized in a critical

Critical Studies: The Merchant of Venice

account that foregrounds the past and continuing dominance of repressive and exploitative ideologies. We should face up to the anti-Semitism of *The Merchant of Venice* precisely because of an imperative need to identify and combat anti-Semitism and all other forms of racial prejudice in our own contemporary world.

The alternative method of interpretation is to propose that all the complexities discovered by modern criticism were from the outset embodied, or implicitly potential, within the Elizabethan text from the outset. It is always difficult to argue for a simplistic imputation of ideological uniformity to a cultural form like drama, which is by its very nature 'dialogic' – composed by the juxtaposition of different and divergent voices – rather than 'monologic' – expressive of a single authoritative voice enclosing a single ideological perspective. The Elizabethan drama was particularly remarkable for such 'polyphonic' – multiple-voiced – discourse because of its generic heterogeneity: where a single play can contain and synthesize the conventions of comedy, romance, tragedy and even history, it is unlikely to offer itself for simplistic, single-minded readings. If the same dramatic narrative can be experienced as comedy by one individual character or group of characters, romance by another and tragedy by a third, then where is the play's ideological centre? If generic diversity suggests discontinuous fortunes for the characters, would that not be likely to produce divergent reactions from members of an audience and disparate interpretations from different readers?

Text and Performance

If we pursue the subsequent history of the play in the theatre rather than in criticism, the evidence points more decisively towards a post-structuralist model of interpretation. By this I mean that changes in the play's theatrical realization can be linked fairly directly to general changes in the understanding and interpretation of the problems the play represents, particularly to the racial problems associated with Shylock, but also to the very idea of a 'Christian' culture being as dedicated to the uninhibited pursuit of wealth as are Shakespeare's Venetians.

It would almost certainly be true to say that had the villain of this particular narrative not been identified as a Jew – had Shylock been characterized, for example, simply as a miser, distinguished morally rather than racially and ethnically from the Venetian Christians – the play would never have produced the critical and theatrical problems that it has. The discordant elements of *The Merchant of Venice* centre on Shylock, and extend from that central figure across other areas of the play. It is perhaps the peculiarly intractable nature of the play's discords which accounts for the remarkable stage history of *The Merchant*, a history containing some extraordinary transformations. In terms of standard Elizabethan attitudes and conventions, Shylock can be assimilated to a definite convention – that of the stage Jew, a variant of the medieval dramatic figure of Vice, embellished with the trappings of contemporary anti-Semitism and the uniform of grotesque farce (red wigs and huge artificial noses). This was, presumably, how the play was performed on the Elizabethan public stage some time in the late 1590s, and before James I in the two recorded court performances of 1605. The play seems not to have been especially popular in its own time. By the early eighteenth century its place in the repertory was being re-asserted, albeit in the form of extremely free adaptation which was the common method in that period of tailoring Shakespearean texts to the needs of the contemporary theatre. In the course of the eighteenth century we can trace a gradual development of the role of Shylock towards the figure of heroic suffering and tragic dignity that became the Romantic movement's standard interpretation of the Elizabethan Jew. The tendency to see Shylock not as a comic villain, but as someone closer to a hero or hero *manqué*, evidently began much earlier than the twentieth century's experience of Fascism. As early as the eighteenth century the role was treated with some measure of tragic dignity. And in the course of the Romantic movement of the early nineteenth century, a serious re-evaluation and reinterpretation of Shylock appeared on both critical and theatrical agendas. Edmund Kean performed Shylock in 1814 as a tragic figure, marking a significant stage in the rehabilitation of the character's dramatic possibilities. When Kean's production first opened in 1814, the critic William Hazlitt was in the audience to register this profound shift of values. 'We have,' he said:

formed an overstrained idea of the gloomy character of Shylock, probably more from seeing other players perform it than from the text of Shakespeare. Mr Kean's manner is much nearer the mark . . . his Jew is more than half a Christian. Certainly, our sympathies are much oftener with him than with his enemies. He is honest in his vices; they are hypocrites in their virtues.[8]

In order for the audience to be capable of sympathy for Shylock, the actor had to approach the role in a fundamentally sympathetic way. The great actor-manager of the later nineteenth century, Sir Henry Irving, was quite clear that 'Shylock is a bloody-minded monster', but equally confident that the role should not be played on that basis: 'you mustn't play him so, if you wish to succeed; you must get some sympathy with him'.[9] Irving invested in his performance of Shylock all the virtues of his characteristically 'noble' style of acting, emphasizing the background of racial persecution and personal humiliation. According to a contemporary reviewer, Irving 'kept a firm front to the last . . . a fine curl of withering scorn upon his lips for Gratiano', as he walked away to die in silence and alone.[10] Irving even interpolated an additional scene, after Jessica's elopement at II.vi, in which Shylock was seen returning to his own house to find it empty and the door locked against him.

It has often been argued that, in addition to reading the text retrospectively in its history, we should try as spectators to view Elizabethan plays in the context of Elizabethan attitudes and prejudices, avoiding the imposition of our own more tolerant and liberal values. An early theatrical attempt to effect such a shift of attention back towards the play's authentic historical character was William Poel's Elizabethan Stage Society production of 1898, which assumed a radical disjuncture between Elizabethan and modern attitudes. In William Poel's view, the play had gradually been twisted from its basic sixteenth-century structure, in which a vindictive alien threatens the serenity of a pleasure-loving European community, to a modern version of which Shylock is the heroic, martyred and persecuted victim of an oppressive society. The play had become, as Poel ironically adapted the wording of the title-page to show, 'The tragical history of the Jew of Venice, with the extreme injustice of Portia towards the said Jew in denying him the right to cut a just pound of the Merchant's flesh, together with the obtaining of the rich heiress by the prodigal Bassanio'.[11] The production appears to have failed to convince, however, for the obvious reason that Elizabethan conventions of racial stereotyping – Shylock was played in a red wig and artificial nose – had become unacceptable to modern liberal opinion. It was precisely such anachronistic liberalism that Poel was trying to combat, but even as early as 1898 it was clearly impossible to read a play about the persecution of a Jew with detached historical objectivity. More recent events such as the twentieth-century Holocaust – a modern tragedy which seemed to confirm very ancient legends of racial persecution – render such an operation of historical distancing out of the question. The kind of cruel amusement which the educated Elizabethan could apparently direct towards Jews can hardly be revived in a culture where the very names of those Second World War concentration camps in which six million of them were annihilated – Auschwitz, Dachau, Belsen – carry such potent symbolic force.

Past and Present

On the other hand, as much recent criticism has convincingly shown, we cannot always be quite so sure as scholars once were of exactly how such 'standard' ideas and prejudices were held by Elizabethan audiences; nor can we confidently attribute those orthodox opinions to Shakespeare or to the plays he wrote. The reading of an Elizabethan play involves both an act of historical imagination – the act of thinking and feeling one's way into a very different historical culture – and an awareness of the ways in which subsequent historical developments and modern beliefs may have changed the play's possibilities of interpretation. Reading in this dialectical way, it becomes possible to recognize within an Elizabethan play potentialities which become fully articulate only in modern interpretation. The modern recognition of Shylock as a tragic figure, which is so incompatible with that Elizabethan grotesque with the red wig and the artificial nose, may be a recognition of possibilities historically inscribed into the play. The pervasive conviction, visible across the whole range of critical approaches, that *The Merchant of Venice* needs to be understood as a problem play or tragicomedy, may simply be a result of those cultural changes that have transformed modern attitudes towards the play and its contents. On the other hand, it may be a recognition that the play was genuinely problematical, authentically resistant to simple categorization, from the moment of its first production and circulation in the Elizabethan popular theatre of the 1590s.

1. Venice and Belmont

The entire action of *The Merchant of Venice* is imagined as taking place in one of these two locations: the commercial and financial republic of Venice, a historical place; and the ancestral country seat of Portia's family, Belmont, which is not on the map in the same sense as Venice, but rather exists fictionally, in terms of the conventions of aristocratic romance. The two places are imagined, though not with any great geographical precision, as far distant from one another in space: journeys have to be taken to pass from one to the other. But there is a much greater distance between the two places in terms of their imaginative status within the dramatic fiction: Venice is a real, modern world, dominated by trading and dealing, by commercial and financial transactions; Belmont is a fantasy world, dominated by the past, characterized by the conventions of fairy-tale and legend.

Venice

In Venice the conversation is always of money, trade, entrepreneurial adventure, of ships and cargoes, silks and spices, of debt and credit, risk and fortune, the course of law and the state of justice. At its centre are the Rialto, the 'exchange' where commercial dealings are conducted, and the Duke's court where the trial of Antonio takes place. The play opens with the character of Antonio, the merchant of the play's title, and within a few lines the audience is treated to an elaborate imaginative sketch of his merchandise in its traffic across the oceans: the silks, spices and other luxury goods that Antonio buys from the Far East and ships to Venice and elsewhere to be sold on the market. Although, however, the language of merchandise is a poetry of distance and traffic, of commercial activity and the international circulation of commodities, the character of the merchant is as remote as could be imagined from the pragmatic acumen, entrepreneurial decisiveness and business confidence that could be expected to stand at the centre of such a financial operation. Antonio is not a sharp opportunistic capitalist but a gentle figure of melancholy and sadness: not thrustingly entrepreneurial but shy and withdrawn, not a repository of trustworthy commercial confidence but an individual deeply inhibited by a condition of extreme anxiety.

Antonio's opening words express nothing of his 'merchantly' status, but speak only of the dissipating and distracting effects of melancholy sadness, the weariness of depression, and a curious sense of self-alienation:

> *In sooth I know not why I am so sad.*
> *It wearies me, you say it wearies you;*
> *... And such a want-wit sadness makes of me*
> *That I have much ado to know myself.*
>
> (I.i.1–2, 6–7)

It is hard to imagine a great maritime commercial empire built by characters such as this. It is only in an effort to cheer Antonio up that Salerio and Solanio fill in the social and economic context of Antonio's commercial livelihood: his sadness, they suggest, must be connected with the risks of mercantile investment, where very large amounts of venture capital have to be expended on an enterprise for it to be profitable. In order to maximize profit, Antonio is obliged to spread his resources as widely as possible, producing the risk of over-extension if several vessels were to miscarry. Later we learn that with the additional burden of the loan to Bassanio, Antonio has indeed over-extended his capital and ironically, the disasters depicted by Salerio and Solanio are precisely, we discover as the play unfolds, the risks Antonio has most reason to fear. Here, though, he indicates that his depression has nothing to do with the anxieties of commercial risk: it is purely personal, and he is not prepared to share the secret with his companions.

We are thus introduced to this great financial and commercial centre of Venice via a merchant who is preoccupied with anything but his merchandise. At the heart of the Venetian trading empire stands a shy, diffident, anxious individual, who is deeply preoccupied with private thoughts, naïvely reliant on his own economic security, and suffering from a deep crisis of identity: 'I have much ado to know myself' (I.i.7). Despite the attempts of his companions to link private anxieties with economic risk –

> SALERIO *Your* mind *is tossing on the ocean* ...
>
> (I.i.8)

> SOLANIO ... *had I such* venture *forth,*
> *The better part of my* affections *would*
> *Be with my* hopes *abroad.*
>
> (I.i.15–17, my emphases)

– Antonio resists any definitive mercantile categorization of his identity – 'my merchandise makes me not sad' (I.i.45) – and slides away from the attempt to place him in the position suggested by the play's title, at the centre of Venetian economic and social life. This begins to seem even more remarkable, as we shall see in the next chapter, when we learn that Antonio appears to be the only member of the community of Venetian Christians who actually is a merchant: there is no indication that Bassanio, Gratiano, Salerio, Solanio and Lorenzo live by trade, or indeed by any other kind of work. They are simply 'gentlemen' who live easily and well on wealth of unexplained origin. Antonio is de-centred not only from Venice, but also from his own social group within the international Venetian community.

We soon, however, learn exactly where Antonio's life *is* centred. He maintains the role of melancholy disaffection –

> ANTONIO   *I hold the world but as the world, Gratiano,*
> *A stage where every man must play a part,*
> *And mine a sad one.*
>
> (I.i.77–9)

– towards all his Venetian acquaintances – Salerio, Solanio, Gratiano and Lorenzo – apart from Bassanio, in whose company he suddenly becomes talkative, positive, outgoing. The basis of his sadness, then, is clearly his relationship with Bassanio, and the prospect of Bassanio's departure for Belmont.

> ANTONIO   *Well, tell me now what lady is the same*
> *To whom you swore a secret pilgrimage,*
> *That you today promised to tell me of.*
>
> (I.i.119–21)

The precise nature of Antonio's friendship, or love relationship, with Bassanio requires detailed discussion, and will be addressed in Chapter 2. For the moment we will concentrate our analysis on the general characteristics of Venetian society and culture. Antonio poses his question in the language of courtly love, with its familiar religious overtones: Bassanio has proposed a 'pilgrimage', a sacred passage to a holy site, as the nature of his quest to win Portia. Bassanio shifts the metaphor into the nostalgic glamour of ancient mythology, identifying Portia as the golden fleece and her suitors as so many Argonauts:

> BASSANIO   *In Belmont is a lady richly left, . . .*
> *Her name is Portia, nothing undervalued*

> *To Cato's daughter, Brutus' Portia;*
> *Nor is the wide world ignorant of her worth,*
> *For the four winds blow in from every coast*
> *Renownèd suitors, and her sunny locks*
> *Hang on her temples like a golden fleece,*
> *Which makes her seat of Belmont Colchos' strond,*
> *And many Jasons come in quest of her.*
>
> (I.i.161, 165–72)

At first glance this substitution of a classical for a Christian metaphor seems an appropriate means of extolling Portia's personal qualities: she is both the holy shrine of a religious pilgrimage, and the legendary object of a mythical quest, because of her 'wondrous virtues'. The obvious difference between pilgrimage and quest is, however, that the latter, with its image of the golden fleece, draws attention to Portia's wealth as a primary focus of Bassanio's attention, and opens to the reader the possibility of interpreting his pursuit as an exercise in fortune-hunting as well as a pilgrimage of love. Terms such as 'nothing undervalued' and 'worth' seem more like moral celebrations than economic valuations, but 'richly left' can only mean that Portia is the heiress to a large fortune. In any case I have of course taken the speech out of context, since it does not appear as a direct reply to Antonio's question, but follows a long, perhaps rather prolix and circumlocutory conversation about money.

BASSANIO   *'Tis not unknown to you, Antonio,*
            How much I have disabled mine estate
            By something showing a more swelling port
            Than my faint means would grant continuance.
            Nor do I now make moan to be abridged
            From such a noble rate; but my chief care
            Is to come fairly off from the great debts
            Wherein my time, something too prodigal,
            Hath left me gaged. To you, Antonio,
            I owe the most in money and in love,
            And from your love I have a warranty
            To unburden all my plots and purposes
            How to get clear of all the debts I owe.

                                        (I.i.122–34)

Bassanio approaches the question of Portia through a financial assessment of his creditworthiness, as if his initial consideration is not to gain a beautiful, loving and virtuous wife, but to settle all his debts by acquiring her fortune. Bassanio has accumulated debts, mainly from Antonio, in the course of sustaining a lifestyle of conspicuous consumption and display which he couldn't afford – 'showing a more swelling port / Than my faint means would grant continuance' (I.i.124–5). His behaviour has been 'prodigal' both in the sense that he has sought to establish a social and economic status through borrowed money, and that so far he has failed to hit the kind of jackpot which would justify the investment of his financial backers. What Bassanio describes to Antonio here is not so much a courtship suit as a business plan. Given this prior context of financial analysis, it becomes impossible to read Bassanio's language of romantic quest in the innocent manner proposed by the conventions of romance:

> BASSANIO   *O my Antonio, had I but the* means
>   *To hold a* rival place *with one of them,*
>   *I have a mind presages me such* thrift
>   *That I should questionless be* fortunate.
>   (I.i.173–6, my emphases)

All the key words in this speech can be read within the discourse of romantic courtship: 'means' being the basic minimum requirement for mounting the enterprise, 'rival place' signifying a place among the rival suitors, 'thrift' usually in Elizabethan English meant simply 'success', what happens when you 'thrive', and 'fortunate' could suggest 'in receipt of the gifts of fortune' in a very general way, 'happy and blessed' rather than merely 'successful'. The context already discussed requires, however, that we also read those words in their economic sense: where 'means' simply signifies financial credit, 'rival place' suggests commercial competition, 'thrift' indicates not success but sound financial management, and 'fortunate' can be understood quite literally as 'in receipt of a fortune'.

The implicit relationships between economics and romance, money and love, lie – together with Shylock – at the very heart of this play's critical and theatrical problems. Do we, for example, assume a natural incompatibility between the language of love and that of money? Do we presuppose that a courtship quest is an activity essentially nobler than a search for wealth? Or that marriage sought for financial gain as well as personal fulfilment is at best compromised, at worst corrupt? Do we find ourselves convinced, having identified the economic dimension of Bassanio's discourse, that his preoccupation with wealth degrades the purity of his motives in seeking Portia's hand in marriage? If we do assume and presuppose positive answers to all these questions, we are only responding to cultural norms that have been dominant for centuries in our society, ever since, in the course of the seventeenth century, the notion of marriage as either a loose sexual union or an arranged property settlement, gave way to the new idea of 'companionate marriage', which assumes the free and equal choice of both partners. And, whatever the general social conditions of English domestic customs in the 1590s, as a cultural form, the idea of marriage as free romantic choice rather than a parentally arranged property settlement was certainly dominant in the popular drama. The new idea of marriage was also endorsed by the cultural conventions of romance. From the outset of its popularity in the early Middle Ages, romance evolved in opposition to dynastic and property marriage: it was a fiction of adultery, in which passion disrupts social arrangements. Gradually romance became domesticated until it could be smoothly incorporated into companionate marriage. If we expect the motives of love to be based on high principles and idealized sentiment, and to minimize or occlude the economic conditions of marriage, then we are only responding appropriately to the conventions of romance.

If this is a standard modern view of the relationship between love and money, is it also necessarily an appropriate way of reading *The Merchant of Venice*? We have no choice but to read the literature of the past in the light of our own contemporary ideology, but this can be done either naïvely – using the past as a mirror which obediently reflects back to us our own assumptions and convictions – or self-consciously – where we identify our own ideological context, and recognize to what extent that context modifies our reading of the past. We need to read both contemporaneously and historically at the same time. When we bring the fiction of the past into present consideration, it becomes assimilated to the conditions of contemporary culture. But the past is also another country, where they do things differently; to read historically is often to acknowledge the cultural difference of the past, its strangeness, the discontinuities that separate 'their' experience from 'ours'.

We need, then, in interpreting the relationship between love and money in Shakespeare's Venice, to consider the possibility that our sense of incompatibility between the two did not then exist, or at least did not always apply.[1] To merge the associations of courtship and economics in a single language may seem to us productive of irony, because we presuppose a radical difference between the two. Yet to the Elizabethan playgoer it may have seemed a perfectly appropriate connection between love as a romantic partnership and marriage as a social institution. In appealing to his relationship with Antonio, Bassanio speaks of 'love' and 'money' as aspects of the same thing: 'To you, Antonio, I owe the most in money, and in love' (I.i.130–31). Both Antonio's willingness to give or lend money, and Bassanio's sense of indebtedness, can be read as direct expressions of love. The romantic/religious pilgrimage of courtship and the economic/mythological quest for fortune may also have seemed unproblematically to be aspects of the same enterprise, an entirely proper and laudable occupation for a young sixteenth-century gentleman. In his anecdote about the two arrows, Bassanio defines the project to Antonio as analogous rather than contrary to a commercial enterprise, a 'hazard' comparable to the risk of Antonio's trading business. The luxurious lifestyle of conspicuous display, based on borrowed capital, which Bassanio has assumed need not, again, necessarily be seen as morally reprehensible. Such elaborate displays of wealth on the part of an élite have always been very widely regarded, in many types of social organization, as a social obligation, and they were certainly considered as such by the Elizabethan aristocracy and gentry. If we are disposed to interpret the term 'prodigal' as a negative valuation, we need to remember the biblical parable of the prodigal son, which is frequently alluded to in the play: a narrative which can be read as justifying the prodigality of the child who wastes everything, rather than the unremarkable service of the child who loyally adheres to the family business.[2]

Belmont

We need to go further into the play and into some of its contexts to pursue this problem. One preliminary internal context is provided by the relationship between Venice and Belmont. The first impression we get as the play's location shifts from one place to another (I.ii in modern editions) is one of contrast. We move from a world occupied entirely by men (Shylock's daughter Jessica is the only female inhabitant of Shakespeare's Venice) to one dominated by women. Although Portia speaks here of her dependence on masculine power, operating through the conditions of her father's will, she is also literally 'lord' and 'master' of her own house, estate, property and wealth (see III.ii.167–8). In terms of the play's overall narrative structure, this situation of female power lies in a temporary limbo between Portia's subservience to her father when alive, and her eventual renunciation of authority to the man she is destined to marry; and since even during that temporary

7

respite from the direct pressures of masculine power, she has to adhere to her father's prescriptions governing the method of her marital choice, it could be argued that Portia is never truly free. This narrative synopsis does not, however, accurately describe the impression Portia makes on readers and audience, nor account for the kind of power she assumes in the trial scene, where her intervention is the essential pre-condition of a successful narrative resolution to the play's moral and ideological problems.

At the basic narrative level, she confesses her situation to be one of irritating dependence:

PORTIA   *O me, the word 'choose'! I may neither choose who I would nor refuse who I dislike, so is the will of a living daughter curbed by the will of a dead father.*

                                                (I.ii.21–4)

In Belmont, then, we encounter a strong sense of family as obligation. Parental authority bears upon the child even after the individual occupants of that authority have died. In Belmont, experience of the present is framed within that strong responsibility to the past: the language of present conversation echoes the presence of those who are no longer here. None the less, despite Portia's awareness of the strength of her own 'will' – desire, inclination, independence – her acceptance of the conditions of her father's 'will' – his last will and testament – indicates a spirit of obedience to the past, to family, to the law, to parental and masculine authority.

Already the geographical distance between Venice and Belmont seems to have its counterpart in sharp cultural difference. In Venice most of the characters don't even seem to have fathers, or at least never mention them: the lives of Antonio, Bassanio and the Venetian gallants operate in a world of nuclear individuals free from any family dependence or obligation. Where characters do have fathers – as in the cases of Jessica and the clown, Launcelot Gobbo – their relationship to paternal authority is characterized by abuse and desertion, by anything but filial obedience. In the comic scene between Launcelot and his father (II.ii), the clown expresses attitudes of mockery towards his father's affliction, playing on the blind, elderly man an easy practical joke of deception and mistaken identity. The case of Shylock's daughter Jessica re-enacts at the narrative level this scene of irreverent dramatic mockery between father and son, rejecting her father completely, abandoning and robbing him to elope with the Christian Lorenzo. The context there is of course at least theoretically different, since Jessica's rejection of her Jewish cultural inheritance is broadly applauded by all the Christian characters; and it is the dutiful model of filial piety, Portia herself, who secures for the 'undutiful' daughter (at Antonio's suggestion) the inheritance of all Shylock's wealth. But this narrative element certainly operates to confirm the general context of family disintegration which seems to be the norm in Venice.

The virtual absence of an older generation also strengthens the impression that Venice is a world without a past, one in which present experience and future aspiration flourish in a rootless, dislocated medium of perpetual contemporaneity. People live between the immediate security of what they have already gained, and the optimistic hyper-reality of what they hope to acquire in the future. This virtual imprisonment of consciousness within the immediate moment is clearly exemplified, as we shall see, in the trial scene, where the entire ruling élite of Venice and a courtroom full of lawyers seem incapable of remembering any law enacted earlier than the day before yesterday. Why does it take the intervention of Portia to recall the statute about conspiracy on the part of aliens? Apparently because Venice has literally forgotten its own past: the state has invested everything in the constitutional liberties of a modern commercial republic, and forgotten older and cruder codes of political self-defence without which its freedom cannot survive.

Belmont is steeped in the past, not only in terms of Portia's obedience to its prescriptions, but in the manner of their implementation.

NERISSA *Your father was ever virtuous, and holy men at their death have good inspirations. Therefore the lottery that he hath devised in these three chests of gold, silver, and lead, whereof who chooses his meaning chooses you, will no doubt never be chosen by any rightly but one who you shall rightly love.*

(I.ii.26–31)

Nerissa is shown by the outcome to be entirely correct: the casket-choice does indeed produce for Portia the right suitor. The sense of improbability in this fantasy – that chance is not arbitrary accident, but providential determination – arises only from the mixing of genres: it is not at all improbable within the context of a romance or folk-tale narrative, where the subordination of chance to meaningful design is precisely what the reader or spectator is trained to expect. The sense of improbability arises simply because the play did not begin in Belmont, but in Venice, that relatively realistic modern world of commerce and finance, debt and credit. If that is our first impression, it will prove in the long run to be mistaken, since Belmont's fairy-tale magic will eventually be required to restore imaginative order to a Venice that has pursued its own kinds of reason and justice to the brink of chaos.

Venice and Belmont

These terms of contrast between Venice and Belmont have formed the basis of much critical discussion of *The Merchant of Venice*. In theatrical realizations, productions have often emphasized the assumed contrast in terms of design and visual spectacle. The relationship between Venice and Belmont in performance needs to be considered in more detail, and will be looked at in Chapter 5. The basic point to grasp is that in the Elizabethan theatre, where the stage employed no scenery or visual means of identifying place, Venice and Belmont would have looked to the spectator exactly the same. Let us look again at the shift from Venice to Belmont, assuming the hypothesis of similarity rather than difference.

Portia's opening words actually echo directly the words of Antonio with which the play opens:

PORTIA *By my troth, Nerissa, my little body is* aweary *of this great* world.

NERISSA *You would be, sweet madam, if your miseries were in the same abundance as your good* fortunes *are; and yet for aught I see, they are as sick that surfeit with too much as they that starve with nothing.*

(I.ii.1–6, my emphases)

We inevitably recall Antonio's 'It wearies me', and 'I hold the world but as the world, Gratiano' (I.i.2 and 77). Nerissa's dramatic function of cheering up her melancholy mistress parallels the role performed by Salerio and Solanio: they suggest that Antonio's imperilled fortune gives him every reason to be sad; Nerissa suggests that Portia ought to be cheered by the thought of her own good fortune.

That initial hint to the effect that Venice and Belmont may be considered as analogous societies, contingent rather than contrary moral worlds, perhaps even separate territories of the same realm, is intensified by a system of parallels and similarities, often lying slightly beneath the surface of the play's language. Antonio describes himself as a figure of stable and secure economic confidence, in control of his own destiny, while Portia protests against her lack of freedom to choose. And yet as the action of the play makes clear, Antonio's confidence is illusory, and his destiny subject to the same arbitrary chances as Portia's. The difference is not in the general condition, but in the necessary acknowledgement of chance as choice seen from another perspective.

But the most significant parallel between Venice and Belmont lies in the concepts of risk and hazard, which are continually identified and cross-referenced across the two locations by the use of a common language. The lottery by which Portia's husband is to be chosen is a game of 'hazard', in which both the suitor (who will either win or lose all hope of future marriage) and Portia take an enormous risk. Despite Nerissa's assurance that the casket-choice is guaranteed to reconcile accident and design, some element of risk must enter into the dramatic emotions of the play. Suppose the wrong suitor chooses rightly? Suppose someone were to cheat? Thus life in Belmont is governed by hazard, in exactly the same way that life in Venice is dominated by risk – the perils of financial disaster entailed in Antonio's merchant ventures, and the dangerous prodigality of the type of personal relationship, such as that between Antonio and Bassanio – in which one partner is prepared to risk everything for the sake of the other. The same moral affirmation of the virtue of 'prodigality' is of course inscribed on to the leaden casket which contains Portia's portrait. The other two caskets, gold and silver, with their respective slogans – '*Who chooseth me shall gain what many men desire*', and '*Who chooseth me shall get as much as he deserves*' (II.vii.5 and 7) – are calculated to tempt the chooser with an ethic of acquisition and self-interest, where the leaden casket invites compliance with the morality of risk, in which the player hazards everything on the chance of a single throw. Bassanio's ritual meditation before making his choice establishes a correct system of relationship between the apparent and the real, show and substance, physical beauty and moral worth, and his final selection of the slogan on the lead casket – '*Who chooseth me must give and hazard all he hath*' (II.vii.9) – enfolds the romantic idealism of Belmont with the personal and economic risk-taking of Christian Venice. At this point Venice and Belmont cease to look like two separate worlds, appearing rather as linked departments of the same enterprise, united by a common morality.

In the context of Belmont and the romance conventions governing dramatization of the casket-choice, Bassanio is the unquestionable hero of the moment, preferred by the lady, favoured by fortune, granted the privilege of the third choice which always in such narratives fulfils the pattern and produces success. In the wider context of the play, however, there are other possible ways of viewing Bassanio, some of them far less indulgent and sympathetic than his fairy-tale performance of the hero's

11

function. We may, for example, recall from the opening Venetian scene the fact that what Bassanio risks in attempting the casket-choice is nothing of his own, but the borrowed property of Antonio. The merchant who has so far done all the giving, risking and hazarding is about to fall victim to Shylock's bond, which will require him to give again for Bassanio – this time with his life. To pursue these more complex layers of meaning will involve a broader consideration of the play's economic preoccupations, which will be addressed in the next chapter.

Our comparison of Venice and Belmont has suggested that the two locations are not after all counterpoised in antagonism, but more deeply interlinked into a common social and ideological structure. It would probably be true to say that in criticism of the play the assumption of their difference is everywhere predominant. This orthodox argument was expressed concisely by W. H. Auden, with particular reference to different conceptions of time:

The action of *The Merchant of Venice* takes place in two locations, Venice and Belmont, which are so different in character that to produce the play in a manner which will not blur this contrast and yet preserve a unity is very difficult ... But Belmont is related to Venice though their existences are not really compatible with each other. This incompatibility is brought out in a fascinating way by the difference between Belmont time and Venice time. Though we are not told exactly how long the period is before Shylock's loan must be repaid, we know that it is more than a month. Yet Bassanio goes off to Belmont immediately, submits immediately on arrival to the test of the caskets, and has just triumphantly passed when Antonio's letter arrives to inform him that Shylock is about to take him to court and claim his pound of flesh. Belmont, in fact, is like one of those enchanted palaces where time stands still.[3]

This argument seems very persuasive. Time seems to operate quite differently in each of the two locations. Antonio's bond with Shylock expires within three months: yet no sooner has Bassanio arrived in Belmont and immediately passed the test of the three caskets, than news arrives that the debt remains unpaid, and the penalty is to come into effect. In Venice, time exerts a real and tangible pressure on human existence, signified clearly by the time-limits placed on loans. In Belmont, time seems rather to stand still, or to move forward through symbolic moments such as a suitor's exercise of choice. In a world dominated by ritual, time is discontinuous rather than linear, since the transition enacted by the moment of choosing effects a rite of passage from one state to another. We observe two of Portia's suitors, the Princes of Morocco and Arragon, undergo an abrupt transition from hopeful aspiration to abject disappointment, from absolute liberty of choice to self-imposed renunciation of all hopes of marriage. As is appropriate to this time-scale, the ritual moment of choosing is what occupies stage-time (the long speeches of Morocco and Arragon have often been considered too prolix for the modern stage, but are entirely appropriate to a process of ritual): both the before and after of that moment disappear into insignificance for the audience. Portia would like to delay the moment of Bassanio's choosing, in order at least temporarily to normalize their relationship:

> PORTIA *I pray you tarry, pause a day or two*
> *Before you hazard . . .*
> *I would detain you here some month or two*
> *Before you venture for me.*
>
> (III.ii.1–2, 9–10)

But the moment of choice, which can split the world inexorably into a lost past and an unachieved future, must be taken. Bassanio, as it happens, chooses correctly. But that successful choice does not restore the normality of time, since Bassanio is abruptly transformed by a rite of passage from the hopeful suitor to the complacent victor; anxious hope is suddenly transformed into eternal happiness. Time progresses by these seismic upheavals, these abrupt discontinuities of linear process. In Venice, by contrast, according to Auden's argument, time operates by the more familiar succession of hours, days and months, which advance inexorably indifferent to human interests: there can be no delaying of the term of Shylock's bond. One way of understanding Portia's role in the trial scene is to see her intervention as the successful substitution of Belmont-time for Venice-time: the temporal dimension of ritual and magic, of sudden transformations and rites of passage, is imposed upon the clock-bound world of Venetian law and commerce.

In fact, what Auden has done here is to mistake the dimension of time as it is understood by Shylock as generally applicable to Venetian culture as a whole. Such a conception of time as gradual linear progress and sequence belongs appropriately with Shylock's type of financial dealing, entailing the careful counting of days and months for the purposes of calculating interest and determining the foreclosure of unpaid loans. For the Venetian Christians, by contrast, time operates in exactly the same way as it does in Belmont: qualitatively rather than quantitatively, by quantum leaps of discontinuity rather than gradual progression, because their time is interrelated with the profession and morality of risk and hazard. The Venetian merchant lives between the dislocated states of immediate success, future anticipation and the danger of absolute disaster, just like the romance figures of fairy-tale Belmont. Antonio's wealth is, according to Salerio, subject to the same unpredictable seismic upheavals:

> *. . . but even now worth this,*
> *And now worth nothing?*
>
> (I.i.35 – 6)

Bassanio's account of his indebtedness to Antonio provides an equally vague conception both of time and money: he has owed Antonio everything (however much that is) for as long as he can remember (however long that may be), and hopes to repay everything not by the slow and patient accumulation of wealth, but suddenly, by a wished-for success in the risky and exciting adventure of his quest for Portia. Had Shylock been standing by, he would automatically have reached for calendar and interest tables to calculate the correct rate of interest. Antonio falls victim to that tyranny of time precisely because, in keeping with the rest of Christian Venice, he simply does not understand time as the moneylender conceives it. Certainly his precipitate collapse from financial security and economic competence into bankruptcy and peril of his life offers the image of an abrupt temporal discontinuity as violent and disorientating as anything that happens in Belmont.

In most respects, I am suggesting, Venice and Belmont are represented as contiguous or analogous rather than radically distinguished places. There are much bigger gaps of culture, race, religion, business ethics and language between Venetian Jews and Christians than any barrier that separates Christian Venice from Belmont. Bassanio, despite his relative poverty, is never considered as less than an appropriate suitor for Portia's hand, and since Portia is in any case in love with him, the barrier between them is composed purely of inherited obligations and responsibilities to paternal authority. 'O these naughty times' says Portia, 'Puts bars between the owners and their rights.' (III.ii.18–19). But all she means is that since Bassanio already 'owns' her by virtue of her love for him ('One half of me is yours, the other half yours', III.ii.16), it seems unjust that their union should be prevented by the barriers of an inhospitable age. At the end of the play all the Christian characters confidently take possession of Belmont, now Bassanio's house, as if it were little more than their country retreat, awaiting the owners' arrival at the end of a social season. This is not the conquest or acquisition of an alien place, but simple occupation of what has always been rightfully 'theirs'.

2. Economics and Sexuality

The third scene of Act I completes the tripartite configuration of the play's structure – Christian Venice/Christian Belmont/Jewish Venice – by introducing Shylock. Shylock's first words are about money – 'Three thousand ducats' (I.iii.1) – and in this opening conversation with Bassanio he fulfils the stereotypical role of the Jewish moneylender. As I have already shown, there are within the play's history of critical and theatrical reproduction divergent possibilities of interpretation in relation to Shylock. Let us consider here what first impressions an unprejudiced reader or spectator, encountering Shylock immediately after the previous scenes, would be likely to form of him.

Shylock: First Impressions

Shylock's language is initially all about money, the terms and conditions of loans and Antonio's creditworthiness. Bassanio is clearly irritated first by his insistent repetitions –

> SHYLOCK *Three thousand ducats, well.*
> BASSANIO *Ay, sir, for three months.*
> SHYLOCK *For three months, well.*
> BASSANIO *For the which, as I told you, Antonio shall be bound.*
> SHYLOCK *Antonio shall become bound, well.*
>
> (I.iii.1–6)

– and then by Shylock's reference to Antonio as 'a good man', which Bassanio interprets as a slight – 'Have you heard any imputation to the contrary?' (I.iii.13). Shylock's riposte – 'My meaning in saying he is a good man is to have you understand me that he is sufficient' (I.iii.14–16) – is a highly characteristic remark: first in that it is painstakingly literal, carefully defining terms as if anxious to avoid misunderstanding; second in that it seems to propose the indicator of financial sufficiency as a measure of goodness. The literal quality of Shylock's speech is a feature often noted.[1] It is as if Shylock finds metaphor dangerously unstable, since it allows for the possibility of multiple meanings. The usurer prefers his professional relations with his clients to be framed within a legalistic precision of phrase. Shylock's adherence to the morality of what Thomas Carlyle later called the 'cash-nexus' (a 'bond of cash', meaning men bound to one another only by bonds of money and exchange) is demonstrated by his careful calculation of Antonio's resources, an elaborate indication that for him the matter is purely a question of money. Under pressure from the eager Bassanio, who invites him to dinner, Shylock drops his guard and voices a language of racial exclusiveness:

Yes, to smell pork, to eat of the habitation which your prophet the Nazarite conjured the devil into. I will buy with you, sell with you, talk with you, walk with you, and so following; but I will not eat with you, drink with you, nor pray with you.

(I.iii.31–5)

That manifesto of cultural difference prepares the way for Antonio's entrance, and Shylock's first major speech – marked by a shift from prose to verse – in which he expresses the complex inter-relations of race, religion and economics:

> *How like a fawning publican he looks*
> *I hate him for he is a Christian;*
> *But more, for that in low simplicity*
> *He lends out money gratis and brings down*
> *The rate of usance here with us in Venice.*
> *If I can catch him once upon the hip,*
> *I will feed fat the ancient grudge I bear him.*
> *He hates our sacred nation and he rails*
> *Even there where merchants most do congregate*
> *On me, my bargains, and my well-won thrift,*
> *Which he calls interest. Cursèd be my tribe*
> *If I forgive him.*

(I.iii.38–49)

Here then, within the first few pages or minutes of Shylock's appearance in text or on stage, he has exhibited all the characteristics attributed to his race and profession by the many hostile witnesses represented in the play. Shylock is preoccupied by money; he sees his relations with other human beings exclusively in terms of the cash-nexus; he adopts an attitude of exclusiveness in his social and domestic life, shunning contact with those regarded as 'unclean' by his religion; he hates all Christians, and particularly Antonio, from a mixture of cultural and economic animosities. The vindictive malice which comes to the surface on Antonio's entrance – 'If I can catch him once upon the hip, / I will feed fat the ancient grudge I bear him' (I.iii.43–4) – can easily be assumed as implicit in all Shylock's words and actions. It can be read both as referring backwards – explaining his careful calculations of Antonio's 'sufficiency' (perhaps Shylock is not searching Antonio's credit-worthiness, but looking for an advantage over him), and forwards – to the implicit malevolence of the 'merry bond' (I.iii.170). It is even possible, tracing a series of buried metaphors through Shylock's speech, to find the plot of the flesh-bond almost fully formed in Shylock's imagination. Though he refuses to share food with the Christians – 'Yes, to smell pork . . .' (I.iii.31) – he cherishes the idea of 'feed[ing] fat' (I.iii.44) his appetite for revenge. When the flesh-bond is proposed, Shylock actually compares the relative market values of human and animal meat:

> *A pound of man's flesh, taken from a man*
> *Is not so estimable, profitable neither,*
> *As flesh of muttons, beefs or goats.*
>
> (I.iii.162–4)

Piecing these images together produces an alarming sub-text which makes Shylock's initial greeting of Antonio with the odd phrase 'Your worship was the last man in our mouths' (I.iii.57) seem positively cannibalistic in implication.

Shylock: A Modern Reading

But here we need to 'tarry a little', to adapt Portia's famous phrase from the trial scene. The Shylock I have just described is certainly there in the text. But there is another Shylock there too, equally implicit in the dramatic context, narrative action and poetic language of the scene. Shylock's first words are about money because Bassanio is seeking to borrow money from him. Shylock is here being constituted by others as the calculating usurer, rather than spontaneously defining himself in that role. Bassanio's irritability springs, we know, from his impatience to fund his project rather than from any high-principled economic or racial animosity. He is borrowing to satisfy his own needs, but it is Antonio who 'shall become bound' – all the responsibilities and penalties of the bond attach to him, all the benefits to Bassanio. It is true that Bassanio is in this respect complying exactly with Antonio's instruction to 'Try what my credit can in Venice do' (I.i.180) but, given Antonio's highly public moral stand against usury, Bassanio by approaching Shylock is surely dragging his friend into a delicate ethical compromise. His credit, Antonio urges, may be 'racked even to the uttermost' (I.i.181) to acquire what Bassanio needs; but that image of torture asks to be applied uncomfortably to Antonio's body as well as to his credit balance.

This context of Christian self-interest and even hypocrisy – it is morally inconsistent to take advantage of a financial service you regard as morally pernicious – colours the depiction of Shylock differently. His irritating mannerisms become symptomatic of a perfectly legitimate resistance to the pressures exerted on him by men who will normally have nothing to do with him. When Shylock declares his credit-search of Antonio's means to be adequate for the purpose – 'I think I may take his bond' (I.iii.26) – Bassanio responds indignantly: 'Be assured you may' (I.iii.27). 'Be assured' here is a mere device of rhetorical insistence, suggesting that Shylock is being insolent to question Antonio's financial competence. Shylock's reply is exact: 'I will be assured I may' (I.iii.28) – i.e. that he has a perfect right to establish the security of the proposed loan, since it needs to be 'assured' (cf. modern 'insured') against the possibility of loss. In this reading, the exchange between the two men is beginning to look less like Christian civility and enthusiasm pitted against Jewish calculation and malice, and more like the dignified resistance of a persecuted minority to the high-handed hypocrisy of those who wish both to despise and make use of their services.

Shylock's cultural exclusiveness is declared within the same context – Bassanio would not normally invite him to dinner. The detailed stipulations of religious observance within a particular faith always seem irrational to those of a different faith: the Jewish taboo against pork is the basis of countless anti-Semitic jokes, although historically Christianity has had its own corresponding, equally arbitrary, taboos in relation to food. But Shylock's punctilious definition of exclusiveness as applicable to certain private activities ('I will not eat with you', I.iii.34) and not to other more public ones ('I will buy with you', I.iii.33) is perfectly in line with the multicultural constitution of Venice, which permits independent private belief and custom in the context of an open involvement in and compliance with the general conditions of social life. That republican constitution was far more tolerant than the parallel conditions of Shakespeare's England, where there was no freedom of speech, thought or worship for Jews (or, of course, Catholic Christians). It is a principle embodied in the constitutions of modern democratic societies, and more strongly affirmed in the more recent concept of a multicultural society. The modern reader, familiar, for example, with the complexities involved for Muslims or Sikhs in negotiating the liberties and constraints of Western democracies, is unlikely to find anything exceptionable in Shylock's statement of cultural principle.

The first reading I offered of this scene could be described as a normative interpretation, which accepts a certain permanent consensus of values, shared between Christian Venice, Shakespeare's England and our own modern societies, enabling the reader to identify naturally with Antonio, Bassanio and Portia, and to encounter the Jew, as they do, as an alien. The second reading depends on a theoretical acknowledgement of cultural difference: of the fact that both horizontally, in terms of cultural diversities within a particular social formation, and vertically, in terms of the cultural changes that take place in history and modify the reading of past literature, there are *legitimate* differences of ideology, racial and ethnic culture, and religion, within any multicultural society. Within this type of reading, we could not 'naturally' feel an imaginative hostility towards Shylock because he is Jewish, speaks in a different accent or dialect, and holds different religious and economic opinions. Of course that acceptance of cultural diversity does not entail the endorsement of malice, vindictiveness, criminality or pathological hatred, since these qualities are subversive of the constitutional balance that permits contradictory belief-systems to co-exist. We may accept the rights of Muslims to think, speak and worship in their own way, but we object to them proceeding, albeit sincerely, in the light of those beliefs, against the life of another citizen, since the same constitutional tolerance protects the life of the one and the beliefs of the other. But we are at least likely in a 'multicultural' reading of *The Merchant of Venice* to interpret Shylock's malice differently.

Shylock's hatred of Antonio is expressed in personal, economic, racial and religious terms. Shylock's inveterate hatred of Christianity envelops Antonio in a history of persecution and resistance. It is because Antonio 'hates our sacred nation' that Shylock hates him as a racial and religious duty: 'Cursèd be my tribe / If I forgive him' (I.iii.48–9). This fundamental conflict between religions also has a history of Christian aggression in its economic aspect, since Antonio does not restrict his hostility to verbal and physical abuse, but extends it into business dealing: 'He lends out money gratis and brings down / The rate of usance here with us in Venice' (I.iii.41–2). The sense of personal injustice derives from the intensely personal and public way in which Antonio has conducted this anti-Semitic campaign against usury.

> SHYLOCK   *Signor Antonio, many a time and oft*
> *In the Rialto you have rated me*
> *About my moneys and my usances.*
> *Still have I borne it with a patient shrug,*

> *For sufferance is the badge of all our tribe.*
> *You call me misbeliever, cut-throat dog,*
> *And spit upon my Jewish gaberdine,*
> *And all for use of that which is mine own.*
> *Well then, it now appears you need my help.*
> *Go to then. You come to me and you say,*
> *'Shylock, we would have moneys,' you say so,*
> *You, that did void your rheum upon my beard*
> *And foot me as you spurn a stranger cur*
> *Over your threshold, moneys is your suit*
>
> (I.iii.103–16)

This description, if true, is an account of persecution, to which we could respond with equanimity only if we shared Antonio's prejudice. The public slights heaped upon Shylock by Antonio may be aimed primarily at his business ('my moneys and my usances'), but they are received as personal insults and racial indignities ('my Jewish gaberdine', 'sufferance is the badge of all our tribe'). The latter metaphor draws attention to the badges that Jews were obliged to wear – in Venice, a yellow 'O' – as the distinguishing mark of their racial otherness. The verbal and physical abuse visited on Shylock by Antonio is justified not by the requirements of legitimate business competition, but by that insignia of racial inferiority. Not only does Antonio not question the truth of Shylock's protest, he endorses it, accepts and vindicates his role as persecutor, and threatens to continue the same campaign of personal victimization. In response to Shylock's very reasonable questions – 'Hath a dog money? Is it possible / A cur can lend three thousand ducats?' (I.iii.118–19), Antonio promises only to continue his vicious vendetta of racial hatred:

> *I am as like to call thee so again,*
> *To spit on thee again, to spurn thee too.*
>
> (I.iii.127–8)

And although Shylock has already shown himself vigilant for any advantage he can secure over Antonio, it is the latter who first introduces the idea of a financial transaction sealed in enmity rather than friendship:

> *If thou wilt lend this money, lend it not*
> *As to thy friends, for when did friendship take*
> *A breed of barren metal of his friend?*
> *But lend it rather to thine enemy,*

> Who if he break, thou mayst with better face
> Exact the penalty.

(I.iii.129–34)

That language of hostile and taunting challenge flows directly from Antonio's aggressive persecution of Shylock, not from the Jew's inveterate malice against the Christian. Certainly that inveterate malice is there, and contextualizing it against a background of racial prejudice and persecution does not make it any the less malicious. We can try to explain, but not explain away, the rooted antagonism that evolves into murderous violence as a strategy of counter-persecution, the violent defensive resistance of the underdog driven to the limit by ill-treatment. But it would be merely a sentimentalization of Shylock to play down his malice by reference to a racial history of victimization. He may not seriously believe that the bond will become forfeit, but malice can be embodied just as definitely in fantasy as in action, in desire as in performance. The person who dreams of cutting out his own enemy's heart cannot be cleared of vindictiveness by reference to the historical or legendary sufferings of his tribe.

None the less, the reading which takes into account modern democratic attitudes towards race, and towards political and religious liberty, produces an interpretation of Shylock significantly different from the reading which presupposes instinctive prejudice as a 'natural' approach. On the other hand, Antonio's reference (in the last speech quoted) to the relations between money and friendship, which invokes a set of ideas very remote from modern assumptions and beliefs, draws attention to the importance of a historical reading alongside the contemporary interpretation. We cannot really understand either Shylock or the play without examining more closely sixteenth-century attitudes towards usury and commerce.

Shylock: A Historical Reading

The significance attributed to Shylock within the play (as distinct from the various meanings conferred on him by critical interpretation) consists largely of a certain relationship between ethnicity and economics, between racial and religious difference, and financial behaviour. The necessity for a historical perspective on the play is nowhere more apparent than in this matter of economics. A clear distinction is drawn in *The Merchant of Venice* between the respective commercial activities of Shylock and Antonio, and underlying that distinction is a clear moral

21

separation, in sixteenth-century thought, between different kinds of business dealing which in the modern capitalist economy would be very difficult to separate. This apparently absolute moral distinction rests on a sharp contrast between the two characters, which in a paradoxical way draws them together into a certain relationship of affinity. Although Antonio clearly belongs to the Christian community, he and Shylock tend to face each other as individuals with a common identity. There is even an analogy in the matter of race, since while most of the Venetian Christians display anti-Semitism of a cultural kind, consisting mainly of racist humour and routine contempt, Antonio's racial hostility is, as we have seen, much more active and concrete. It takes the form of a deliberate and determined commercial rivalry, based on a principled objection to the practice of usury.

It is commonly assumed by readers of the play that Shylock's fault is to charge excessive interest on loans. This misapprehension rests on an understandable misreading of the word 'excess' (I.iii.59), which actually means simply what we mean by 'interest'. Shylock himself, however, rejects that particular term – he speaks of his 'bargains' and his 'well-won thrift', which Antonio calls 'interest' (I.iii.48). Shylock lends money at interest and on security of property, land or person. Antonio does not object to Shylock because he charges too much interest: he objects to the idea that interest can be charged, as it would be today, from the moment of the loan. He does not object, however, to the adding of interest to the principal (the sum borrowed) after the repayment date has passed, which is why he is able to reconcile himself to Shylock's bond, which operates on this latter system rather than on the basis of usury.

The difference is similar to that between a bank loan, on which you pay interest from the moment the agreement is signed, and borrowing on a credit card, where interest becomes payable only after the repayment date has passed, after the interest-free period has expired. This distinction between different methods of lending money and collecting interest was a key issue in the anti-usury propaganda of the early modern period,[2] though clearly it seems a very fine distinction to us. The distinction is further blurred for us because in the ethics governing the kind of modern economy to which we are accustomed, there is no such moral distinction between usury and speculation, between what would now be called finance and venture capital. To think ourselves into this moral climate we would have to imagine a society in which financiers, and bank and building society managers, were hated and reviled, while company shareholders and speculators were regarded as irreproachably beneficial members of society. It is entirely possible comprehensively to admire or dislike all of these functionaries, but their activities are far too deeply intertwined in the modern capitalist economy to permit any clear ethical distinction between them.

In *The Merchant of Venice*, however, there is a fundamental, structural, ethical distinction between what Shylock and Antonio respectively do for a living. Antonio *trades*: he buys luxury goods from the East and West Indies, such as silks and spices, and sells them on the market in Venice. Antonio's speculative ventures involve *risk* (as the plot ultimately demonstrates), while Shylock's do not, since the usurer is bound to get either his money plus interest, or whatever security (such as the debtor's property and goods) has been bound over to him. The defaulting debtor became a criminal: so the law (in the case of Elizabethan England, a statute of 1571 making usury legal and open) could be seen as protecting the moneylender, where the speculative merchant would be risking everything in hazardous ventures which might at any moment turn to disaster.

These moral objections against usury were medieval in origin. A properly functioning feudal economy (in which land is exchanged for labour, and goods produced for use) has no place for money at all, let alone moneylending. The existence of moneylending on a large scale is a sure economic indicator that the feudal economy is breaking down, and giving way to capitalistic financial dealing. Medieval theology condemned usury as a sin, while the religious writers of the Protestant Reformation, Luther and Calvin, accepted it as a necessity. Antonio in *The Merchant of Venice*, although a leading member of a new social class, the speculative entrepreneurial trader, has commercial ethics identical to those of an old class, the landowning aristocracy.[3]

The play asks its audience to consider the difference between usury and speculative commerce not only in economic terms, but in the light of moral values. The business of the merchant is identified with friendship, that of the usurer with enmity. The former is regarded as disinterested and selfless, the other grasping and selfish. Antonio's trade is seen as an activity which enriches not only himself, but the life of the community as a whole. The exchange of money for goods is seen as fertilizing, enriching, fruitful, while the exchange of money for money is assumed to be sterile, wasteful, profitless.

> *... for when did friendship take*
> *A breed of barren metal of his friend?*
> (I.iii.130–1)

To take interest on a loan, to make money multiply (or 'breed' as in Shylock's analogy with Jacob's sheep) by the taking of interest, is seen as essentially an act of enmity rather than friendship. Friendship gives without exacting reward or threatening punishment; enmity charges interest and binds the creditor to legally enforceable penalties on failure to repay.

Merchant and Jew

As I indicated earlier, Antonio doesn't confine himself to sermons and exhortations against usury, or even to kicking and spitting on Shylock's person: he conducts an active, practical campaign against the usury he despises. Shylock hates him, not merely because he is a Christian, 'But more, for that in low simplicity / He lends out money gratis and brings down / The rate of usance here with us in Venice' (I.iii.40 – 42). Antonio cuts out the moneylenders by means of interest-free loans, thereby depressing the interest rate by reducing demand. But he goes further than this, to the extent of deliberately rescuing defaulting debtors from the usurer's contract. Antonio later admits that Shylock has come to hate him not from motiveless malignity, but because of this real and systematically inflicted commercial injury.

> *He seeks my life. His reason well I know:*
> *I oft delivered from his forfeitures*
> *Many that have at times made moan to me.*
> *Therefore he hates me.*
>
> (III.iii.21–4)

Both Shylock and Antonio are isolated from the remainder of the cast. Although the play, as the title indicates, is all about commerce, trade, financial dealing and exchange, only two of the leading characters appear in fact to be directly involved in business. Portia is a wealthy heiress, a landed proprietor. Bassanio lives on credit and by speculation on the marriage market. Gratiano, Solanio and Salerio are not identified as merchants; if anything, their opening conversation with Antonio, in which they describe how they would feel if their fortunes were at risk on the high seas, suggests that they are not. They are either parasites, hangers-on of the rich, gentlemen of independent means, or possibly (given their eager acquaintance with stock exchange gossip) some equivalent of the modern-day financial speculator. Lorenzo is, like Bassanio, poor and without means; his livelihood is secured by the abduction of Jessica, who brings as her dowry first her father's more portable property, and ultimately his entire fortune, expropriated at Antonio's suggestion by the court of Venice. The remaining characters are all servants or rulers.

In this way Shylock and Antonio are differentiated from the other characters, and placed (in different but related ways) outside the play's central community. They represent two opposed business ethics and two opposed moralities within the world of Venetian commerce. They are business rivals and competitors, enemies of trade and financial dealing. And in some strange way, they are very much alike. Antonio is clearly from the outset isolated from the community of Christians, of which Bassanio is a natural member. Like Shylock, Antonio does not like masques and feasting. While the rest of the world is carefree and irresponsible, his role is to play a sad part. His melancholy, his loneliness, his sense of difference and isolation, all link him to his mighty opposite, Shylock. The play opens with Antonio's supposedly mysterious and inexplicable melancholy. The reason for this sadness is in fact perfectly obvious: he loves Bassanio (only loves the world for him', II.viii.50); he is not a lover of women, indignantly rejecting suggestions that he may be in love with one; and he is pointedly left out of the otherwise universal celebrations of marriage at the play's conclusion. His melancholy, then, is a response to the frustration of an unrequited love (homosexual, though not necessarily entailing a physical relationship) for Bassanio. When in the opening scene all the other characters leave the two men alone together, Antonio offers himself to Bassanio in naked though equivocal language: 'My purse, my person, my extremest means / Lie all unlocked to your occasions', (I.i.138–9). 'Purse' and 'person' are linked in a very suggestive metaphor, as Antonio offers the 'extremities' of both fortune and body to his friend. Antonio's generosity and self-sacrifice could be identified as the means by which he can hope to hold the affections of a friend whose emotional life is always likely to be invested elsewhere: Bassanio is, after all, a healthy red-blooded heterosexual, who seems to display if anything a certain callousness and insensitivity to the sexual emotions of his friend.

In his *Divina Commedia* Dante placed usurers and sodomites (homosexuals) in the same circle of Hell. Usury seemed to the medieval mind an unnatural way of doing a natural thing: that is, it was considered natural to create wealth and to prosper, but unnatural to do so by lending money at interest. The view that it was unnatural to make money, to 'breed' money, as the usurer does, could be found in Aristotle's *Ethics*, and this was connected with a similar moral distinction between heterosexual and homosexual love. To create wealth by the exchange of commodities for money was considered natural, and aligned with heterosexual love; each process could produce a third thing (profit or children) different from either. But money, as Aristotle insisted, is a *barren* metal, which cannot breed by itself. We find this economic controversy expressed in the play, when Shylock refutes a stock argument against usury by claiming that money can in practice, like Jacob's sheep, breed like a living thing. Thus, by virtue of his sexual difference as an isolated homosexual man, Antonio stands out from the norms of Venetian society just as sharply as Shylock is contra-distinguished against the norms of Christian Venice.

In two important passages of reported action, closely juxtaposed within a single scene (II.viii), these two characters are polarized into a dialectical relationship of identity and opposition.

> SOLANIO   *I never heard a passion so confused,*
> *So strange, outrageous and so variable*
> *As the dog Jew did utter in the streets:*
> *'My daughter! O my ducats! O my daughter!*
> *Fled with a Christian! O my Christian ducats!*
> *Justice! The law! My ducats and my daughter!'*
> (II.viii.12–17)

> SALERIO   *I saw Bassanio and Antonio part;*
> *Bassanio told him he would make some speed*
> *Of his return; he answered, 'Do not so.*
> *Slubber not business for my sake, Bassanio,*
> *But stay the very riping of the time . . .'*
> *And even there, his eye being big with tears,*
> *Turning his face, he put his hand behind him,*
> *And with affection wondrous sensible*
> *He wrung Bassanio's hand; and so they parted.*
> (II.viii.36–40, 46–9)

The loss, in each case, of wealth and of affection, is identical: having eloped with a Christian, Jessica is lost to her father, and a share of his wealth with her; Antonio is assisting Bassanio towards a relationship which will inevitably introduce some estrangement of their accustomed intimacy, by contributing a substantial part of his fortune to the enterprise. The merchant and the usurer are polarized into a diametrical opposition which suggests both analogy and difference. If we read the comparison in terms of opposition, we find a distinction between a man who puts love on a level with money ('My ducats and my daughter!'), who cannot separate human from material loss, and a man who, having already given, in financial terms, enough to render him vulnerable to bankruptcy and execution, and having yielded up his love to the embraces of a woman, can yet find it possible to give more. There could be no clearer distinction between the man who cannot distinguish money from love, and the man who is prepared to 'give and hazard all he hath' (II.vii.9) for the sake of a love that can never bring him compensation or restitution.

Yet, when inspected more closely, the linking of Shylock and Bassanio yields a dimension of parallelism together with the sense of contrast. The relationship between Antonio and Bassanio, expressing itself through giving and indebtedness, lending and gratitude, is no more free from mercenary considerations than that between Shylock and Jessica. Love and money are just as closely interconnected, though with different emphases corresponding to different commercial moralities: Shylock is committed to an ethic of personal and financial possession – in the later scene with Tubal he wishes his daughter 'dead at my foot, and the jewels in her ear! Would she were hearsed at my foot, and the ducats in her coffin!' (III.i.80–82) – and Antonio to a morality of infinite generosity. But this distinction, though real enough, is (like that between usury and merchant capitalism) a comparatively fine distinction within a larger shared compliance with the necessary interpretation of love and wealth, money and affection. The witnesses who report these twin scenes invoke them as representative of clear moral difference between Shylock, the 'dog Jew' (II.viii.14), and Antonio, than whom 'a kinder gentleman treads not the earth' (II.viii.35). But unless we as readers or spectators are predisposed to accept that relative valuation, it is surely more reasonable to see the two predicaments as parallel personal tragedies of loss. Both men are isolated, culturally or sexually, in their grief. As Antonio turns his back on Bassanio he decorously hides his unmanly sorrow, yet at the same time places himself in a characteristic posture of homosexual intercourse.

In another dramatic juxtaposition, the two appear as counterparts rather than opposites:

SHYLOCK *I'll have my bond! Speak not against my bond!* . . .
SOLANIO   *I am sure the Duke*
       Will never grant this forfeiture to hold.
ANTONIO *The Duke cannot deny the course of law,*
       For the commodity that strangers have
       With us in Venice, if it be denied,

> *Will much impeach the justice of the state,*
> *Since that the trade and profit of the city*
> *Consisteth of all nations.*
>
> (III.iii.4, 24–31)

Shylock here stands for justice, the law, and requires his legally permitted compensation for Antonio's non-performance of their contract. Antonio, despite the fact that it is his own life and property that are forfeit, is fully in agreement with Shylock as to the justice of the usurer's cause. Antonio may speak the Christian language of compassion and mercy (though he showed little of either to Shylock), while Shylock appeals to the simple poetic justice of the Mosaic law. But both are in complete agreement on the validity of that internationalist law of Venice ('the commodity that strangers have / With us') which regards all races as equal.

Within the context of Venetian law the problem remains insoluble, except, that is, by the forfeiture of Antonio's life. Dramatically, the plot here reaches a stalemate. The power to resolve the problem seems quite unavailable within the ethical and legal codes governing Venetian life and commerce. Venice has to look to its *alter ego*, Belmont, for rescue and salvation. Meanwhile the polarization of Antonio and Shylock as counterparts rather than opposites dominates the central section of the play. Antonio is perhaps at his most impressive when, in the trial scene, his language rises to the biblical dignity and tragic intensity of Shylock's:

> *I am a tainted wether of the flock,*
> *Meetest for death.*
>
> (IV.i.114–15)

Since a 'wether' is a castrated sheep, Antonio is again calling attention to his sexual difference, which isolates him as much as his status as victim. The Christian, whose ritual persecution of Shylock consistently strove to place the Jew on a level with animals, now finds himself turned into a lamb in a Jewish ceremony of sacrifice. It is not for nothing that the title by which we know the play seems originally to have been interchangeable with another: in the Stationer's Register it is referred to as ' "The Merchant of Venice", otherwise called "The Jew of Venice" '.

3. Jews and Christians

The opening three scenes of Act I, with their respective introductions of Antonio, Portia and Shylock, indicate by their accumulating comprehensiveness the method of the play's dramatic narrative. From the beginning of the play to the end there is a continual shuttling back and forth from Venice to Belmont, until the two final, complementary scenes close the pattern: Portia visits Venice for the trial (IV.i) and Christian Venice resettles in Belmont (V.i). The narrative of the caskets proceeds through three scenes (II.i, II.vii, II.ix) until the fourth, concluding casket scene (III.ii) in which Bassanio's successful choice concludes and resolves this strand of the play's plot. The same scene reveals Antonio's danger, and in III.iv Portia leaves for Venice, reappearing in disguise at the trial. During the relatively slow evolution of the single Belmont narrative, with its long and verbose ritual scenes, the rapidly shifting, changeable world of Venice presents a panorama of varied city life: the clown Gobbo with his father (II.ii) and with Jessica (II.iii); the preparations for a masque that does not take place (II.iv), and for the abduction of Jessica (II.vi), the consequences of which are then reported by Solanio and Salerio (II.viii).

The main narrative movement in Venice, however, concerns Shylock, who appears through a sequence of scenes which dramatize and connect his losses of Launcelot (II.v) and Jessica (III.i) with the news of Antonio's losses (III.i); his conducting of Antonio to prison (III.iii); and his moment of dominance in the first part of the trial scene (IV.i). As Portia's defence of Antonio swings the balance of power away from him, Shylock is once again constituted in the role of victim and disappears from sight (almost indeed from memory) before the end of IV.i. Act V restores the threatened Christian community back to the security and harmony of Belmont.

In that series of scenes from II.v through to the trial, we see Shylock in a range of contexts additional to his first appearance with Antonio and Bassanio. We see him domestically, with servant and daughter; we see him professionally, in company with the only other Jew (apart from Shylock and Jessica) brought into the play, his fellow-usurer, Tubal; and we see him judicially, in the position of a legal plaintiff with the law on his side. Throughout these scenes the linked concerns of race, religion and economics are continually interwoven.

'Loss upon loss'

The parallel desertions of Launcelot and Jessica are connected by a common language. As master, Shylock is identified by his servant as a 'devil':

GOBBO   *To be ruled by my conscience, I should stay with the Jew my*
         master who, God bless the mark, is a kind of devil; and to run
         away from the Jew, I should be ruled by the fiend, who, saving
         your reverence, is the devil himself. Certainly the Jew is the very
         devil incarnation; and in my conscience, my conscience is but a
         kind of hard conscience to offer to counsel me to stay with the
         Jew.

                                                              (II.ii.19–26)

Initially the Jew is only a metaphorical devil, as compared with the 'fiend', the 'devil himself', who counsels Gobbo to commit a crime (deserting his service). On reflection, however, the true devil, who is advocating flight from the Jew, seems preferable to the metaphorical devil, the Jew himself; hence Gobbo concludes that the Jew is a devil worse than the Christian devil himself. Jessica implies a similar contrast:

JESSICA   *I am sorry thou wilt leave my father so.*
           Our house is hell, and thou a merry devil
           Didst rob it of some taste of tediousness.
                                                      (II.iii.1–3)

Launcelot here is only a mock devil, the clowning Vice from a morality play and as such is preferable to the real devil, her father, who presides diabolically over the 'hell' of their house. Launcelot defines the transition from Shylock's service to Bassanio's explicitly in racial, cultural and religious terms:

The old proverb is very well parted between my master Shylock and you,
sir. You have the grace of God, sir, and he hath enough.

                                                              (II.ii.138–40)

The 'old proverb' in question was 'the grace of God is gear enough' (i.e. is all one needs to possess). Launcelot splits it between Bassanio and Shylock: the former as a Christian is in receipt of divine grace; Shylock, who has 'enough' in terms of wealth, is as a Jew denied the much more valuable commodity of Christian grace. Jessica also resolves the dilemma between filial duty and personal inclination by deciding between the moral claims of Judaism and Christianity:

> *Alack, what heinous sin is it in me*
> *To be ashamed to be my father's child.*
> *But though I am a daughter to his blood,*
> *I am not to his manners. O Lorenzo,*
> *If thou keep promise, I shall end this strife,*
> *Become a Christian and thy loving wife.*
>
> (II.iii.16–21)

Jessica's elopement is more than an escape from an authoritarian father with a distasteful profession and more than a romantic flight from the tediousness of a sober house. It is also a desired renunciation of her own Judaic culture in favour of Christianity.

The dramatic conventions operating within these scenes, the broad popular comedy of Launcelot's appearances, and the romance of Jessica's, scarcely permit to reader or audience any complexity of awareness, any possibility of a 'multi-cultural' reading. We are invited to laugh at the clown's castigation of his tyrannical master, and to feel sentiment for the beautiful young Jew's rejection of her authoritarian father. Thus in both cases and in both genres, the unquestioned priority of Christian belief justifies acts of civil disobedience – absconsion from service and filial desertion – which would in any realistic context be acknowledged as at best immoral, at worst criminal and sinful. No alternative view is either stated or implied within the particular generic context. The correctness of either character's choice of Christianity in preference to Judaism, as cultural inheritance and domestic environment, is not questioned.

These scenes of comic and romantic presentation prescribe the manner of Shylock's next appearance (II.v), in which he abundantly demonstrates all the characteristics of the established stereotype. Shouting and rebuking, Shylock fulfils the roles of tyrannical master and authoritarian parent; rattling keys and dreaming of money-bags, he exemplifies the mean spirit of the miser. By insisting that Jessica keep his house tightly locked, its windows firmly shut against the sounds of the expected festivity, Shylock shows himself both repressive towards his daughter, and puritanically averse to the celebrations of carnival.

> SHYLOCK   *I am bid forth to supper, Jessica.*
> *There are my keys. But wherefore should I go?*
> *I am not bid for love, they flatter me,*
> *But yet I'll go in hate to feed upon*
> *The prodigal Christian . . .*
>
> (II.v.11–15)

> *What, are there masques? Hear you me, Jessica:*
> *Lock up my doors; and when you hear the drum*
> *And the vile squealing of the wry-necked fife,*
> *Clamber not you up to the casements then,*
> *Nor thrust your head into the public street*
> *To gaze on Christian fools with varnished faces;*
> *But stop my house's ears, I mean my casements;*
> *Let not the sound of shallow foppery enter*
> *My sober house . . .*
>
> (II.v.27–35)

> *Drones hive not with me;*
> *Therefore I part with him, and part with him*
> *To one that I would have him help to waste*
> *His borrowed purse.*
>
> (II.v.46–9)

Shylock's echoes of the complexities of earlier scenes – such as the reminder of Christian opportunism and hypocrisy in 'I am not bid for love, they flatter me' (II.v.13) are lost in the petty and comic vindictiveness of his hatred: he will reluctantly dine with the Christians to consume what he can of their wealth ('to feed upon / The prodigal Christian'); and he will gladly accept Launcelot's transfer to Bassanio's service since that will place an additional drain on Bassanio's resources, and in turn on Antonio's fortune: 'help to waste / His borrowed purse'. The occasional glimpse of a cultural dignity, such as the Miltonic

> *Let not the sound of shallow foppery enter*
> *My sober house . . .*
>
> (II.v.34–5)

– or of a private world of domestic affection in

> *Jessica, my girl . . .*
> (II.v.15)

– is simply occluded beneath the graphic delineation of a multiple stereotype: grasping miser, hard-dealing master, bullying parent, unsociable Jew.

> *Do as I bid you; shut doors after you.*
> *Fast bind, fast find,*
> *A proverb never stale in thrifty mind.*
> (II.v.51–3)

'I am a Jew'

In a later scene (II.viii) the controlling perspective of romantic comedy, which prescribes that the elopement of Jessica be seen only from the perspective of its beneficiaries, erupts into a cruder form in Solanio's description of the 'dog Jew' and his uncontrollable passion. And it is Solanio and Salerio who subsequently encounter Shylock, with that 'outrageous' passion still strong in him. Initially this scene (III.i) promises to continue in the same comic vein, where even the reported loss of one of Antonio's ships becomes an occasion for some obscure jokes about rhetorical speech (III.i.1–15). Solanio repeats the identification, already made by Launcelot and Jessica, of Shylock as a devil, emphasizing the element of race:

Let me say amen betimes lest the devil cross my prayer, for here he comes in the likeness of a Jew.

(III.i.19–20)

But then, in a startling dramatic reversal, Shylock himself appears and, in appearing, fractures all these confining stereotypes in an extraordinary outburst of dramatic passion, which not only directly confronts the collusion of Solanio and Salerio in his daughter's abduction, but also throws a wider challenge to the racial hostility of Christian Venice that endorses their actions. That challenge has continued to speak beyond the particular dramatic situation, to extend and reverberate far beyond the specific conditions of Shylock's Venice or Shakespeare's England.[1] The power of its indignation derives from Shylock's insistence on identifying race as the root of Christian Europe's antagonism towards Jews. The passion of grief arising from the loss of his daughter, so casually and cruelly mocked by Solanio and Salerio –

There is more difference between thy flesh and hers than between jet and ivory . . .

(III.i.35 – 6)

– focuses into a passion of anger against Antonio: 'He hath disgraced me and hindered me half a million, laughed at my losses, mocked at my gains, scorned my nation, thwarted my bargains, cooled my friends, heated mine enemies, and what's his reason?' (III.i.49–53). Out of Shylock's resentment at this recollected history of indignity, abuse and economic warfare, lacerated into particular anger by the personal hurt and humiliation of Jessica's desertion, there evolves a compelling

33

affirmation of human dignity which seems both universal, essentially human, and culturally specific:

I am a Jew. Hath not a Jew eyes? Hath not a Jew hands, organs, dimensions, senses, affections, passions? Fed with the same food, hurt with the same weapons, subject to the same diseases, healed by the same means, warmed and cooled by the same winter and summer as a Christian is? If you prick us, do we not bleed? If you tickle us, do we not laugh? If you poison us, do we not die? And if you wrong us, shall we not revenge? If we are like you in the rest, we will resemble you in that.

(III.i.53 – 62)

There are a number of reasons why this speech should give the impression of an utterance that speaks beyond the world of the play, apparently testifying to a universal humanity. It contains, in the first place, a large-scale moral generalization rather out of keeping with Shylock's normally intensely literal, punctiliously specific mode of speech. In addition, it has also been extensively used, being much quoted, to express exactly such a universalized claim to a common human dignity in the world outside the drama.

But if the speech is examined within its dramatic and poetic context, things are not quite so simple. Certainly the common humanity to which Shylock lays claim is a simple concept: human beings are biologically virtually identical to one another despite the differences and barriers of race, religion and culture. In the earlier exchange, Salerio had asserted that Christian and Jewish flesh are essentially dissimilar, as different as jet and ivory (III.i.35–6). The difference assumed there seems, from the metaphor of 'flesh', to be a basic biological distinction, like that between black and white skin. Yet Salerio clearly intends his definition of difference to be a cultural one, since he is arguing that Jessica, Shylock's own daughter by blood, as a kind of honorary Christian despite her Jewish background, is not composed of the same flesh as her father. Shylock's emphasis is also on the nature of physical existence, but on commonality rather than difference:

Hath not a Jew eyes? Hath not a Jew hands, organs, dimensions, senses, affections, passions? Fed with the same food, hurt with the same weapons, subject to the same diseases, healed by the same means, warmed and cooled by the same winter and summer as a Christian is?

(III.i.53–8)

If all human beings are fundamentally alike, sharing an identical physical nature in the form and operations of the body and its sensory relation to the world, what justification can there be for discrimination between one human being and another on grounds of race or ethnicity?

On the other hand, Shylock is launching his demand for equality of rights and dignity specifically from a position of difference. The statement 'I am a Jew' functions dramatically as a response to the rhetorical questioning of Antonio's motives for his personal enmity, 'and what's his reason?'. Positioned at that point in the dialogue, the statement reads initially as a denial and dismissal of cultural difference: 'Antonio's reason for persecuting me is no stronger than this: I am a Jew.' On the other hand, the statement can also be read affirmatively, as a positive proclamation of cultural identity: 'I *am* a Jew, and as such should not be denied the dignity and toleration to which all men are entitled, and which are particularly appropriate to my race and religion.' The claim to equality must, paradoxically, spring from exactly such an experience of cultural subordination: no one pleads to be treated as a human being – a plea which is then inevitably read as an assertion of humanity – unless they are already being treated as less than one – and therefore conscious of being dehumanized by that treatment. I am a Jew: I am human like everyone else. I am a Jew: I am human, but not like everyone else. I am a Jew: I am not treated as a human being. I am a Jew: I should be accorded a basic human dignity.

In the same way, the logic of Shylock's speech runs in two quite different directions. Underlying it there is on the one hand the Utopian ideal of a universal equality: a fundamental biological kinship between all human beings, which should prescribe parallel values of social, cultural and political equality. Running quite counter to this is a contrary idea: a reductive diminution of all human existence to the lowest possible level. All human beings, including Christians, react in precisely the same way to the same external stimuli: tickling produces laughter, a wound provokes the flow of blood. Antonio's past persecution of Shylock can clearly be identified as a sustained campaign of vengeance against an imputed injury – the 'offence' caused to Antonio's Christian sensibility by the active existence within his business community of an alien, Shylock. Antonio's response to this 'provocation' has been to take revenge by persecution. Why then should Shylock respond any differently to the injuries he has sustained as the object of that persecution?

Just as Shylock's demand for human treatment flows from his expression of cultural difference, so his Utopian pleas for universal equality and religious tolerance are inseparable from a vindictive determination to repay his enemy's injustice in like kind, or better still with 'interest':

And if you wrong us, shall we not revenge? If we are like you in the rest, we will resemble you in that.

(III.i.60–62)

In this way Shylock's passionate self-defence against manifest injustice – the racial abuse of his interlocuters and the abduction of his daughter – modulates into the specific threats against Antonio, and a determination to exact the penalty for the forfeited bond. It should be emphasized, however, that neither Antonio nor the bond is at this point uppermost in Shylock's mind; he is far more concerned with the loss of his daughter.

You knew, none so well, none so well as you, of my daughter's flight.

(III.i.22–3)

In this exchange the Christians mock Shylock's loss, identify the Jew with the devil (III.i.30) and insist that Shylock's daughter does not participate in the corruption of his own flesh (III.i.35–7). Yet Shylock does not mention Antonio, until Salerio brings up the subject of the merchant's losses – 'But tell us, do you hear whether Antonio have had any loss at sea or no?' (III.i.37–9). Immediately the anger provoked by Jessica's desertion finds a new focus:

Let him look to his bond. He was wont to call me usurer. Let him look to his bond. He was wont to lend money for a Christian courtesy. Let him look to his bond.

(III.i.43–5)

'Shall we not revenge?'

There is clearly a crucial link between Shylock's other injuries, such as the Christian conspiracy to steal his daughter – in which Antonio was not implicated – and a longer history of persecution – in which Antonio by his own confession was closely involved. Yet dramatically, that connection seems to be provided from outside, rather than arising directly from Shylock's own processes of thought and feeling. It is articulated in the most graphic way possible by the consecutive, virtually simultaneous entrances of two minor players, 'a Man from Antonio', who summons Solanio and Salerio to Antonio's house (III.i.67–8) and Shylock's fellow-usurer, Tubal, who brings news of Jessica's profligate and expensive pleasures (III.i.70). As the Jews confer, the Christians leave the stage, confirming their identification of Judaism with the devil:

SOLANIO *Here comes another of the tribe. A third cannot be matched,*
unless the devil himself turn Jew.

(III.i.70–71)

In conversation with Shylock, Tubal continues to enforce the connection
between Shylock's losses and Antonio's, between the occasion of injury
and the opportunity of revenge, in an almost comically mechanistic
way; there seems to be no logical connection at all between Tubal's
discontinuous sequence of observations:

I often came where I did hear of her, but cannot find her.

Yes, other men have ill luck too. Antonio, as I heard in Genoa . . .

Your daughter spent in Genoa, as I heard, one night fourscore ducats.

*One of them showed me a ring that he had of your daughter for a
monkey.*

But Antonio is certainly undone.

(III.i.74–113 *passim*)

These very strong dramatic emphases on the provocation of Shylock to
revenge himself against Antonio clearly colour the reader's evaluation
of his motives. Again, the bond would not be there to exploit if Shylock
had not initially entered into it. But if, for example, the play had shown
Shylock obsessively counting days to the expiry of the bond, and vindict-
ively anticipating the fulfilment of his revenge, the dramatic effect
would be very different indeed from this systematic establishing of links
between racial persecution, personal tragedy, economic competition
and the passion of revenge.

*Why there, there, there, there! A diamond gone cost me two thousand
ducats in Frankfurt! The curse never fell upon our nation till now; I never
felt it till now . . . I would my daughter were dead at my foot, and the
jewels in her ear! Would she were hearsed at my foot, and the ducats in
her coffin! . . . Why thou loss upon loss! The thief gone with so much, and
so much to find the thief! – And no satisfaction, no revenge! Nor no ill
luck stirring but what lights o'my shoulders, no sighs but o'my breathing,
no tears but o'my shedding.*

(III.i.76–88 *passim*)

This identification of financial with personal loss recalls Salerio's description of the 'passion so confused' in which Shylock had mourned the
joint loss of money and daughter: 'My daughter! O my ducats!'

37

(II.viii.12). Yet, as we have seen, the intimate connection of financial and emotional concerns is by no means peculiar to Shylock, but appears just as strongly in the language of the Christian characters.[2] It was after all the Christians who stole Shylock's possessions as well as his daughter; and Antonio's final act of revenge at the end of the trial scene is to expropriate Shylock's wealth for the advantage of the runaway daughter and her Christian husband, Lorenzo. The language of Shylock's speech, mingling an ancient note of racial tragedy with the genuine accent of personal bereavement, transcends the easy satire of the Christians against the confusion of wealth and person – 'loss upon loss!' (III.i.84).

The curse never fell on our nation till now; I never felt it till now.

(III.i.77–8)

The ancestral dignity of that generalized memory of historical persecution accentuates and confirms the bitterness of personal grief: 'The curse never *fell* . . . I never *felt* it.' This is the authentic language of tragedy. It touches a depth of feeling most of the Christian characters, with the exception of Antonio and (as we shall see) Portia, never reach. It sets Shylock, at least momentarily, in a position where the casual mockery and superficial abuse of the Christians cannot touch him. It sounds a note which the play's comic music cannot, ultimately, contain, except as a disturbing disharmony, a plangent discord, a tragic tone disrupting the concord of comedy.

4. Law and Power

Shylock's appearances in the play from here until the trial scene, although separated by various other scenes, are in a 'real-time' sense continuous. III.i ends with his injunction to Tubal to 'fee me an officer' to arrest Antonio (III.i.116); in III.iii we see him conducting Antonio with his gaoler back to imprisonment; and Shylock reappears then for the last time in the trial scene proper, IV.i. Thus from the critical dramatic conjuncture discussed above, in which Shylock gives vent to his passionate outburst of tragic feeling and his scathing indictment of racial inequality, his dramatic presence is wholly concentrated on the sustained pursuit of judicial revenge against Antonio.

Structurally, however, the play does not single-mindedly pursue this dominant narrative line, but continues to juxtapose the linear sequence of Shylock scenes (which have now also become the Venetian scenes) with passages of dramatic narrative involving the Christians in Belmont: the final casket scene (III.ii); the scene in which Portia determines to pose as 'Doctor Balthasar' (III.iv); and a comic interlude (III.v) involving the clown Launcelot, Lorenzo and Jessica. At this point in the play, where Shylock has achieved a temporary dominance, Venice and Belmont are polarized against one another in a configuration of extreme opposition. In Venice there are only Shylock, Antonio and the bond: racial conflict, financial competition and the law. In Belmont are Bassanio, Portia and the rest of the Christian community, now incorporating the defector Jessica: cultural integration, economic success and love.

For Love or Money

Venice and Belmont also invade one another, however, with the news of Antonio's disasters reaching Belmont immediately after Bassanio has chosen the correct casket (III.ii.219); and with Portia similarly intervening into the trial scene in Venice (IV.i.163). Furthermore, if we examine each of the two polarized dramatic worlds, we find once again that each discloses a common deep structure of language and ideology. This is nowhere more apparent than in III.ii, the final casket scene. In her opening speech conducting Bassanio to his ritual of choice, Portia identifies the ordeal as a 'venture' (III.ii.10) and a 'hazard' (III.ii.2), thereby linking the conventions of Belmont romance with the values of

Venetian commerce. Bassanio gravitates towards the correct casket via a meditation on the emptiness of appearances which concludes – ironically, in the context of his abundantly stated economic motives – in an ascetic renunciation of the symbolism of wealth, in favour of a commitment to a more fundamental reality, embodied in the casket of lead.

> BASSANIO   *So may the outward shows be least themselves.*
> *The world is still deceived with ornament . . .*
>
> (III.ii.73 – 4)
>
> *Thus ornament is but the guilèd shore*
> *To a most dangerous sea, the beauteous scarf*
> *Veiling an Indian beauty; in a word,*
> *The seeming truth which cunning times put on*
> *To entrap the wisest. Therefore thou gaudy gold,*
> *Hard food for Midas, I will none of thee;*
> *Nor none of thee, thou pale and common drudge*
> *'Tween man and man.*
>
> (III.ii.97–104)

Symbolically gold and silver are associated here respectively with superficial ornament and with commercial exchange. By opting for the 'paleness' of 'meagre' lead, Bassanio rhetorically distances himself from the pursuit of gilded, superficial beauty ('ornament') and from the financial bartering in which silver changes hands. It is also worth noting how easily – in the metaphor of 'ornament' ('the beauteous scarf / Veiling an Indian beauty') which implies that true beauty and the complexion of an Indian are mutually exclusive – Bassanio casually appeals to a sentiment we would today regard as essentially racist.[1]

The overt meaning of this ethical critique of 'ornament' is that Bassanio pursues a deeper truth than superficial beauty, a more substantial reality than mere wealth. The problem is that he is seeking here to separate and distinguish things which have hitherto consistently been integrated into a single world-view, characteristic of all the Venetian Christians. From the outset, the quest for Portia and the pursuit of a fortune have been inseparable elements of Bassanio's motivation. Contextually this factor is strongly emphasized throughout the final casket scene, despite Bassanio's efforts to disengage romantic from mercenary, ideal from material considerations. The motto of the lead casket, '*Who chooseth me must give and hazard all he hath*', may accord with Bassanio's language of renunciation, but also accentuates the seamless unity of Belmont romance and Venetian commerce. The scroll Bassanio finds inside the casket assures him that his prize consists of wealth as well as love: '*Since this fortune falls to you / Be content, and seek no new*' (133–4), where the 'fortune' ('good luck') is both Portia herself and her fortune ('wealth'). Portia in speaking of herself uses the familiar language of wealth and commercial transaction:

PORTIA   *Though for myself alone*
            I would not be ambitious in my wish
            To wish myself much better, yet for you
            I would be trebled twenty times myself,
            A thousand times more fair, ten thousand times
            More rich, *that only to stand high in your* account,
            I might in virtues, beauties, livings, friends,
            Exceed account; *but the full* sum *of me*
            Is sum *of something, which to term in* gross
            Is an unlessoned girl . . .
                        (III.ii.150–59, my emphases)

There is no dissociation here of virtue and beauty from riches and power. Bassanio and his company continue to regard the entire expedition in the light of a financial venture. Bassanio refers to himself as a man who has won a competition, 'one of two contending in a prize' (141). Gratiano, announcing his intention to marry Nerissa, opens up the prospect of a new field of competition: the couples could gamble on their prospects of producing the first male heir: 'We'll play with them, the first boy for a thousand ducats' (III.ii.213–14). Despite his professions of emotional confusion, Bassanio is so acutely conscious that in winning Portia he has acquired her property, that when the visitors from Venice arrive, he immediately adopts the stance of host:

            Lorenzo and Salerio, welcome hither . . .
                        (III.ii.220)

It is of course the hospitable prerogative of the owner to welcome guests to a house. Bassanio has so rapidly appropriated Portia's social authority, slipped so easily into that lordly and patronizing manner, that he displays his own embarrassment with the hasty qualification:

            . . . *If that the youth of my new interest here*
            Have power to bid you welcome.
                        (III.ii.221–2)

Since Portia has formally renounced her authority as mistress of Belmont to Bassanio (III.ii.163–71), this can be read as an appropriate courtesy. But underlining the sense that this is more an arrogation than a voluntary transfer of power, there is in the speeches of Portia a definite implication that Bassanio's success may in some senses be read as her failure, his gain her loss. I will return to this aspect of the representation of Portia in the final chapter. Would not Bassanio seem a more admirable figure if he were to hesitate rather more in his overt and public declaration of himself as lord and master of Belmont, as well as victor in the competition for Portia's hand?

Gratiano is also remarkably prompt in assuming authority, both in relation to his fiancée and to Belmont itself. In a very revealing detail, he assigns Nerissa to look after Jessica:

> *Nerissa, cheer yond stranger; bid her welcome.*
> (III.ii.237)

Gratiano then has very rapidly taken on sufficient social power to command Nerissa, and to extend Bassanio's welcome to the 'stranger' Jessica. But why does Gratiano refer to her as a stranger? Since he took part in her abduction with Lorenzo and Salerio (II.vi), he must know perfectly well who she is. 'Stranger' must therefore be an allusion to her Jewishness, a formal designation of her status as an alien. There is something quite remarkable about Gratiano's declining to greet Jessica, whom he knows, assigning someone else to greet her, denying his acquaintance with her, and overtly calling attention to her cultural difference in the word 'stranger'. Not only does the Christian, with striking rapidity, assume the easy manners of social dominance, he also moves quickly to begin constructing a social hierarchy within Belmont, one in which women and aliens are formally subjugated to masculine predominance. Gratiano establishes his social priorities by shaking hands with Salerio and ordering his fiancée meanwhile to look after Jessica.

Finally, it is Gratiano who confirms the identification of romance and wealth by employing again the image of the golden fleece:

> *How doth that royal merchant, good Antonio?*
> *I know he will be glad of our success;*
> *We are the Jasons, we have won the Fleece.*
> (III.ii.239–41)

Bassanio had originally used this metaphor (I.i.170–72) in reference to Portia's person: 'her sunny locks / Hang on her temples like a golden fleece'. But in that context the image clearly functions to identify the romantic pilgrimage with the quest for fortune, the 'worth' of a beautiful and virtuous woman with the 'fortune' she would bring to her husband.

By linking, through that same image, the economic context of Venice with their 'success' in Belmont, Gratiano confirms the successful romance quest as inseparable from a successful commercial enterprise.

That memorable mythological emblem also acts as a crucial turning point in this scene, as Bassanio's success is suddenly juxtaposed against Antonio's disaster.

> SALERIO *I would you had won the fleece that he hath lost.*
>
> (III.ii.242)

As Gratiano rejoices in the winning of a golden fleece, Salerio reports the loss of Antonio's merchandise, the 'fleece' of wealth which protected him from the cold wind of economic insecurity. Antonio will shortly in the trial scene be describing himself as a 'tainted wether of the flock': the 'royal merchant' has fallen to the position of a sacrificial sheep, waiting to be both 'fleeced' and slaughtered by the butcher Shylock. Bassanio now has the even more embarrassing task of admitting to Portia that he is even poorer than she could have realized, and moreover heavily indebted to Antonio:

> *Gentle lady,*
> *When I did first impart my love to you,*
> *I freely told you all the wealth I had*
> *Ran in my veins – I was a gentleman –*
> *And then I told you true; and yet, dear lady,*
> *Rating myself at nothing, you shall see*
> *How much I was a braggart. When I told you*
> *My state was nothing, I should then have told you*
> *That I was worse than nothing; for indeed*
> *I have engaged myself to a dear friend,*
> *Engaged my friend to his mere enemy*
> *To feed my means.*
>
> (III.ii.252–63)

This confession may be read as a scrupulously honest declaration of the truth. But the manner of its utterance is marked by that prolixity and repetitiveness, that circumlocutory reluctance to come directly to the point, which characterized Bassanio's exchanges with Antonio in the opening scene of the play. It is, in short, the characteristic language of Bassanio's embarrassment. With a touchingly naïve and candid openness, he both accepts all blame and absolves himself of any responsibility for remedy. In the opening scene, he freely admits he has spent all Antonio's money, and can only throw himself on the generosity of his friend. In the later scene with Portia, he freely admits he has huge undisclosed debts, and can only throw himself on the generosity of his fiancée. He then merely waits for Portia to come up with enough money 'up-front' to discharge Antonio from the original debt, which she promptly does, though not without a certain acidity of tone that many critics have found disturbing:[2]

> PORTIA *Bid your friends welcome, show a merry cheer;*
> *Since you are dear bought, I will love you dear.*
> (III.ii.313)

It has been suggested that 'dear bought' refers to Bassanio's debt to Antonio, but such an interpretation is clearly twisting the obvious meaning in order to clear Portia of any unpleasant suggestion that she may be complaining about how much Bassanio is already costing her. In the kind of critical reading I am offering, however, such evidence of resentment in Portia can be read as a welcome sign of legitimate female resistance. It is certainly indisputable that Bassanio has no solution to the problem of his own creating, and automatically relies on Portia to suggest one. Thus there is here another turning point, wherein Portia rapidly moves into the vacuum of Bassanio's will-less inertia, and begins to take the initiative in a series of sharp and peremptory commands:

> PORTIA *Come away,*
> *For you shall hence upon your wedding day.*
> (III.ii.310–11)
>
> *... dispatch all business and be gone.*
> (III.ii.322)

Bassanio's role has thus passed rapidly through a series of mutations. Hitherto he has adopted the active, questing function of the romance hero in pursuit of his desire. For a brief moment, in the first flush of his success, he assumed the dominant role of lord and master of his newly acquired property. The news of Antonio's disaster, followed by Bassanio's confession of poverty and his manifest incapacity for decisive action, cause a kind of collapse in the positive force of his role. Bassanio is now being ordered by his fiancée to draw money from her resources, and to hasten to Venice to repay Antonio's debt. The initiative has imperceptibly passed from Bassanio, and Portia begins to reveal herself as fully capable of taking that initiative – at least temporarily – and exercising it in her own right.

Men and Women

In III.iv we see this happening in Portia's intention to adopt a disguise, and to intervene in Antonio's trial as a lawyer. A number of significant emphases arise from this brief scene. Firstly, Portia and Nerissa are to disguise themselves as men, discarding the assumed passivity of their sex and assuming the freedom to travel alone and to act with decision This transformation is particularly ironic since the men of the play, who bear the cultural insignia of assumed decisiveness and activity, are actually far less positive and capable than the women; yet the women have to disguise themselves as men in order to have access to effective authority. Secondly, Portia, by adopting the persona of Dr Balthasar is clearly planning to intervene in the legal process of Shylock's suit; yet in a previous scene we observed her dispatching Bassanio to Venice with money sufficient to repay the debt. Why does she assume that further intervention will be necessary? Does she not trust Bassanio to handle the matter correctly? Or does she instinctively know, or prophetically anticipate, that the offer of financial restitution will be refused, and that Shylock will take nothing less than his penalty, a pound of Antonio's flesh? In the intervening scene immediately preceding, III.iii, Shylock has appeared to the audience as ferociously determined to exact his forfeit:

> *Tell not me of mercy . . .*
>
> (III.iii.1)

> *I'll have my bond! Speak not against my bond!*
> (III.iii.4)

> *I'll not be made a soft and dull-eyed fool,*
> *To shake the head, relent, and sigh, and yield*
> *To Christian intercessors.*
>
> (III.iii.14–16)

It is abundantly evident from this scene that Shylock is both determined to pursue his suit against Antonio, and confident that the law is on his side. Since he specifically rejects any plea for mercy, and refuses to heed the voice of 'Christian intercessors', it becomes obvious to the audience that Bassanio's mission is unlikely to meet with success. On the other hand, Portia can of course have no knowledge of this exchange. In performance, this problem is not so pressing as it seems to be in the reading of a dramatic text. Frequently in Elizabethan drama a knowledge imparted to the audience is then assumed to be in the possession of a character who could have had no naturalistic access to the information. But whether we assume that Portia is preternaturally intelligent, or guided by an instinct the correctness of which is then demonstrated dramatically in III.iii, the effect is more or less the same: the woman recognizes that the problem facing her husband is more intractable than he suspects, and she clearly believes that the problem cannot be resolved by her husband alone, even armed with her own, apparently infinite, financial resources. Hence she mobilizes her own resources in preparation for her decisive and conclusive intervention into the trial.

Merchant and Jew

In the trial scene (IV.i) Shylock and Antonio confront one another for the last decisive combat. When Portia first arrives, she asks the Duke to identify plaintiff and defendant –

> *Which is the merchant here? And which the Jew?*
> (IV.i.171)

– as if they are virtually indistinguishable protagonists, though they ought to be immediately distinguishable one from another by their dress. Portia's initial inability to distinguish merchant from Jew does, however, emphasize their nominal equality in the eyes of the law. It is precisely that principle of legal equality, constitutionally guaranteed to all citizens of Venice, that has enabled Shylock to pursue his 'strange' and barbaric suit (which of course is quite out of keeping with the liberties of a republican constitution) to such extreme lengths. Salerio reported that Shylock 'doth impeach the freedom of the state / If they deny him justice' (III.ii.278–9); and Antonio himself has admitted that the reputation of Venetian justice would indeed be discredited if Shylock were seen to receive less favourable treatment under the law than Venetian Christians:

> ANTONIO   *The Duke cannot deny the course of law,*
> *For the commodity that strangers have*
> *With us in Venice, if it be denied,*
> *Will much impeach the justice of the state,*
> *Since that the trade and profit of the city*
> *Consisteth of all nations.*
>
> (III.iii.26–31)

Portia identifies Shylock's cause as strange – both unusual, and by implication the work of a stranger or alien – but admits that the law has no power to prevent his proceeding.

> PORTIA *Of a strange nature is the suit you follow,*
> *Yet in such rule that the Venetian law*
> *Cannot impugn you as you do proceed.*
>   (IV.i.174–6)

Despite her allusion to Shylock's alien status in the reference to the 'strange nature' of his suit, Portia in her guise as a lawyer is in a sense purporting to view the combatants with an impartial lawyer's eye, seeing only two individuals who are strictly equal before the Venetian law. This paradox – that the laws of Venetian society permit equally to all individual citizens freedoms which can then be used to deprive other citizens of that same freedom – lies at the heart of the trial, just as it lay at the heart of Shylock's great 'I am a Jew' speech. In that earlier speech, Shylock's insistence on a fundamental human equality is also paradoxical since it is used both to demand equality of human rights, and to justify an equality of privilege in the taking of revenge. As we have seen, this argument is rooted in an acknowledgement of racial identity and cultural difference: 'I am a Jew.' In the trial scene, however, Shylock's specifically alien status does not form part of his own case against Antonio, though it is certainly uppermost in the minds of all the other participants.

The Duke sets the tone immediately by addressing the merchant by his (Christian) name: 'What, is Antonio here?' (IV.i.1), and referring to Shylock by a generic racial title: 'Go one, and call the Jew into the court' (IV.i.14). In his opening address to Shylock the Duke also emphasizes Shylock's alien status, his 'strange' behaviour (despite its strict legality) putting him outside the moral community of Venice:

> DUKE *Shylock, the world thinks, and I think so too,*
> *That thou but lead'st this fashion of thy malice*
> *To the last hour of act, and then 'tis thought*
> *Thou'lt show thy mercy and remorse more* strange
> *Than is thy* strange *apparent cruelty . . .*
>   (IV.i.17–21, my emphases)

The Duke invites Shylock to renounce his position as 'stranger', and to enter the moral consensus of Christian Venice. That ethical community is defined in terms of universal values: if Shylock could be 'touched with human gentleness and love' (25) in observing the merchant's losses, he would be prepared not only to 'loose the forfeiture' (24), but also to cancel part of the original debt. By appealing to the apparent universality of the values of 'human gentleness and love' (25), the Duke, however, unwittingly draws attention to Shylock's otherness. Antonio's misfortunes would, the Duke asserts,

> *. . . pluck commiseration of his state*
> *From brassy bosoms and rough hearts of flint,*
> *From stubborn Turks and Tartars never trained*
> *To offices of tender courtesy.*

(IV.i.30 – 33)

Even non-Christians would feel sorry for Antonio, would be touched by 'human gentleness and love' although they have had no training in civilized graces of 'courtesy'. Members of other racial groups, Turks and Tartars, do not have the benefit of such training. Shylock, as an inhabitant of Christian Venice, can participate in the benefits of its civilization. But of course Shylock, being as much an 'infidel' as a Turk or a Tartar, can just as easily be accused of anti-social behaviour rooted in his racial otherness. The sub-text of this speech therefore becomes clear: if Shylock were fully a member of the cultural and ethical community of Venice, he would not be able to press his cruel and vindictive suit: 'human gentleness', 'love' and 'tender courtesy' would prevent him. If Shylock is not merely pretending to pursue the suit to its fatal end, then his motives are those of a hostile alien, akin to those of 'stubborn Turks and Tartars'. The Duke's final line of appeal contains a quite extraordinary pun:

> *We all expect a gentle answer, Jew.*

(IV.i.34)

– where 'gentle', juxtaposed to 'Jew', comes close enough to 'gentile' (i.e. non-Jew) to clinch the argument. 'Are you', the Duke is asking, 'going to drop this case, or proceed with it? Are you going to behave like a Christian, or a Jew?'

The problem confronting the Duke and the entire Venetian state is that the legal system of Venice simply does not replicate its own sense of moral order. If in the interests of what we would now call free trade no restriction is placed on the limit to which a commercial contract can be used to threaten the life of one of its signatories, then the appeal to a moral dimension transcending the sphere of legal and financial practice can carry little conviction. Shylock's case rests consistently on his right in law, guaranteed by the contract freely entered into by Antonio, and protected by the law of Venice. In prosecuting these rights, Shylock virtually ignores the issue of his Judaism and alien status, despite the continual emphasis of all around him on precisely that point as the crucial element in the case. Apart from the opening reference to his having sworn an oath 'by our holy Sabbath' (IV.i.36), Shylock makes no reference at any point in the trial to his own Jewishness. He makes no mention of the racial persecution he has suffered, nor of the abduction of his daughter and the associated theft of his property. He makes no allusion to his commercial vendetta against Antonio, nor to the latter's overt animosity and financial interference with his business. All these would of course constitute motives of hostility, and perhaps undermine Shylock's case. On the other hand they would, if the court were genuinely prepared to consider both sides of the issue equally, provide a context for a more sympathetic interpretation of Shylock's actions, as they do within the play itself.

Shylock adheres tenaciously to the one salient point which he thinks will win him the case: if the bond is legal, the court must allow him to exact the legal penalty. When questioned as to motive, Shylock simply refuses to answer:

> *You'll ask me why I rather choose to have*
> *A weight of carrion flesh than to receive*
> *Three thousand ducats. I'll not answer that,*
> *But say it is my humour. Is it answered?*
> (IV.i.40–43)

> *. . . So can I give no reason, nor I will not,*
> *More than a lodged hate and a certain loathing*
> *I bear Antonio, that I follow thus*
> *A losing suit against him. Are you answered?*
> (IV.i.59–62)

In this way, although admitting to his personal animosity against Antonio, Shylock suppresses the whole question of motive (and with it all the associated concerns of race and economics with which the drama has been largely concerned). Besides, Shylock asserts, he is doing nothing essentially dissimilar, in claiming his rightful share in Antonio's flesh, to Venetian slave-owners who accept the buying and selling of human flesh in the form of slavery (IV.i.89–100).

Above all, Shylock tries to make his suit a test case measuring the true character of the Venetian constitution. Shylock has sworn

> *. . . To have the due and forfeit of my bond.*
> *If you deny it, let the danger light*
> *Upon your charter and your city's freedom!*
> (IV.i.37–9)

> *If you deny me, fie upon your law!*
> *There is no force in the decrees of Venice.*
> *I stand for judgement.*

(IV.i.101–3)

Again, Shylock's argument is that he, in common with all other inhab-
itants of Venice, possesses equal rights, protected by the republic's
constitution. But the suit can only be regarded as a legal test case
because Shylock, being an alien, is claiming legal compensation from
a Christian citizen. So the demand for universal individual equality is
again launched specifically from a position of cultural subjugation.
Each time Shylock is invited to join the Christian community and
subscribe to its values, the discourse of invitation reminds him of his
unequal cultural status. 'How shalt thou hope for mercy' asks the
Duke, 'rendering none?' (IV.i.88). But mercy is of course the dominant value of the Duke's Christian religion, not of Shylock's Judaism:
'What judgement shall I dread,' is his reply, 'doing no wrong?'
(IV.i.89).

Portia proposes exactly the same solution as the Duke: 'Then must
the Jew be merciful' (IV.i.179). Her eloquent celebration of the virtue of
mercy (IV.i.181–99) is strictly irrelevant, since again it privileges a
specifically Christian set of values:

> PORTIA *Therefore, Jew,*
> *Though justice be thy plea, consider this:*
> *That in the course of justice none of us*
> *Should see salvation.*

(IV.i.194–7)

As a Jew, Shylock could hardly expect, however much mercy he displays
in this case (and as Portia's brusque manner of address – 'Then must
the Jew . . .', 'Therefore, Jew', 'Tarry, Jew' – may forcefully remind
him) ever to see Christian salvation. Portia virtually admits the uncer-
tain relevance of her own rhetoric, since it does nothing to undermine
the legal basis of Shylock's case:

> *I have spoke thus much*
> *To mitigate the justice of thy plea,*
> *Which if thou follow, this strict court of Venice*
> *Must needs give sentence 'gainst the merchant there.*

(IV.i.199–202)

Throughout the first half of the trial Shylock is continually assured that he is an equal in the eyes of the law, and is continually offered the opportunity of renouncing his suit, and embracing the common values of Venetian civilization. But since the offer is always couched in the language and imagery of Christian culture, it never quite succeeds in constituting Shylock as the free and equal citizen of Venice he is theoretically guaranteed by the republic's constitution to be. The Christian culture of Venice is not, in other words, prepared to embrace Shylock's otherness, to concede true equality to his alien status; it will accept him only as a Christianized Jew who is prepared to renounce his race, religion and beliefs along with his legal action against Antonio. This undercurrent of racial inequality is forcibly accentuated by the continual current of racial abuse that follows, quite unchecked by the presiding legal authorities, from Antonio and Gratiano:

ANTONIO   *You may as well do anything most hard*
          As seek to soften that – than which what's harder? –
          His Jewish heart.

                                            (IV.i.78–80)

GRATIANO *Not on thy sole, but on thy soul, harsh Jew,*
          Thou mak'st thy knife keen . . .

                                            (IV.i.123–4)

          O be thou damned, inexecrable dog,
          And for thy life let justice be accused!
                      (IV.i.128–9)

The self-evident criminality of Shylock's proceeding against Antonio's life is here specifically associated with his Jewishness, and the vicious circle of racial hatred – 'The villainy you teach me I will execute, and it shall go hard but I will better the instruction' (III.i.65–6) – continues to revolve. There is a radical disjuncture between the perspective of the modern reader and the reactions of the Christian characters in the drama to Shylock's persistence in his cause. We see a man severely provoked by racial abuse into a course of understandable though illegitimate revenge. They see a Jew whose obdurate persistence in his revenge is demonstrating the justice of their original characterization of him as vicious, cruel and inhuman.

Portia leads Shylock almost to the point of execution with her assurances that his suit is legally unassailable, and then with her famous injunction to pause – 'Tarry a little' – produces a devastating dramatic reversal, which sets the action spinning off in a completely opposite direction. The law giving Shylock the right to exact his penalty is still not questioned, but alongside it Portia produces other statutes which render the exaction of the penalty a criminal offence. These laws, unlike the law protecting the cosmopolitan freedom of commercial exchange, are fundamentally racist in character, since they are designed to protect the Venetian citizen against the competitive actions of racial or cultural outsiders:

> PORTIA *Take then thy bond, take thou thy pound of flesh,*
> *But in the cutting it if thou dost shed*
> *One drop of Christian blood, thy lands and goods*
> *Are by the laws of Venice confiscate*
> *Unto the state of Venice.*
>
> (IV.i.305–9)

The subsequent injunction to cut off no more and no less than 'a just pound' seems to be part of that same law protecting Christian flesh against the non-Christian enemy. To subvert the law that treats all men equally, Portia invokes a law designed explicitly to treat them unequally: if the situation were reversed and Shylock stood in danger of Antonio, the Jew would not be protected against the Christian in the same way as the Christian is protected against the Jew. Finally, Portia reveals her bottom-line defence of Antonio, a conspiracy law, again targeted directly at the outsider:

> PORTIA *It is enacted in the laws of Venice,*
> *If it be proved against an alien*
> *That by direct or indirect attempts*
> *He seek the life of any citizen,*
> *The party 'gainst the which he doth contrive*
> *Shall seize one half his goods, the other half*
> *Comes to the privy coffer of the state,*
> *And the offender's life lies in the mercy*
> *Of the Duke only . . .*
>
> (IV.i.345–53)

Initially then, Portia attempts to resolve the deadlock by appeal to a universal natural law: she elevates the problem from one of law and finance, where there is no rational appeal beyond the justice of contract, to one of universal morality, where the dominant value is mercy and forgiveness. She offers Shylock the opportunity of incorporation into a harmonized political economy where Jews would rationally forfeit their legal rights in the interests of the public good. Shylock's refusal – a resistance in which the determined fundamentalism of religious faith and the stubborn reality of economic forces are joined – renders this solution impossible. Having failed in her attempt at incorporation, Portia openly proceeds to use the power of Christian nationalism against him. Underlying the superficial multiculturalism of that cosmopolitan Venetian law, in which Shylock wholly believed, lies a judicial structure designed to protect Christian Venetian citizens against aliens.

The 'mercy' ultimately offered to Shylock by the victorious Christian community – to keep his life without his property – is a fate described earlier by Antonio as one worse than death. It is one to which he readily consigns Shylock, sharpening that injury with additional demands that can only be interpreted as vindictive:

> ANTONIO *So please my lord the Duke and all the court*
> *To quit the fine for one half of his goods,*
> *I am content, so he will let me have*
> *The other half in use, to render it*
> *Upon his death unto the gentleman*
> *That lately stole his daughter.*
> *Two things provided more: that for this favour*
> *He presently become a Christian;*
> *The other, that he do record a gift*
> *Here in the court of all he dies possessed*
> *Unto his son Lorenzo and his daughter.*
>
> (IV.i.377–87)

The crude phrase 'that lately stole his daughter' and the reference to Lorenzo as his 'son' seem particularly insensitive allusions to the experience we know to be Shylock's deepest tragedy. But the demand that Shylock renounce his religion subsumes the minor insensitivities in a comprehensive and systematic act of cultural violence. By appropriating Shylock's wealth and diverting it ultimately into the Christian economy, and by forcing Shylock into conversion, Antonio has been able to strike a harder blow than any he had ever aimed at the Jewish religion and Jewish business he so bitterly despises. Shylock, meanwhile, is finally proven right: he was never, in the last instance, considered by Venice as anything other than an outsider.

5. The Elizabethan Stage

Before proceeding to discussion of the play's final act, we will consider in this chapter the physical conditions of the theatre in which *The Merchant of Venice* was first performed around 1596–8 and the character of the written text, as known to us through the earliest printed editions, on which those first performances were based. The Elizabethan public playhouse for which Shakespeare wrote was in some ways quite dissimilar to many modern theatres and the plays written for that theatre were shaped specifically for production within its singular architecture. To relocate the plays back into the theatre which originally produced them is often to discover or clarify certain features lost or obscured in the course of their historical development as performance-texts. Those changes are clearly marked in the evolution of the modern Shakespeare edition, which in many ways is quite unlike the early printed text from which it was derived. The first published edition of *The Merchant of Venice*, that of 1600 (of which subsequent early editions, such as that contained in the first collected edition of Shakespeare's plays, published in 1623, were all reprints), can give us a unique insight into possibilities of both performance and interpretation which tend to be suppressed or occluded in the modern Shakespeare edition.[1]

The Elizabethan Theatre

The theatres which began to appear on the outskirts of the City of London from 1576, and in which all Shakespeare's plays received their public performance, were open-air amphitheatres, modelled on existing places of entertainment such as bear-baiting arenas. The typical Elizabethan public playhouse was a circular, open-air building, containing a big platform stage partially covered by a tiled roof. Within a round or polygonal structure the stage occupied a central position. At the rear of the stage stood a flat wall, behind which was the tiring-house (where the actors 'attired') surmounted by a gallery. Thus the rear of the stage was known as the 'tiring-house façade'. The stage jutted out from the front of the tiring-house, where the actors dressed and waited to appear. Exits and entrances were made through two doors in the tiring-house façade; above the doors there was the gallery, in which actors could appear 'aloft'. A roof supported on two columns covered half the stage, and above that was the hut which could contain any machinery needed for lowering actors or props down on to the stage from above. The audience space consisted of a yard in which people had to stand, surrounding the stage on three sides and galleries where seating accommodation was available at a higher price. The audience were thus placed all around the stage, on three sides; some stood in the yard around the stage, and others sat in the tiered galleries that ran around the inside of the theatre's outer wall.

So the kind of theatre in which *The Merchant of Venice* came into being was very different from a typical modern theatre and in its first performances on the stage of the Elizabethan theatre, *The Merchant of Venice* was probably very different from the play you might see performed in such a modern theatre. There are of course many types of theatre in existence today – studio theatres, theatres-in-the-round, and so forth – but by 'typical' I mean the sort of theatre, based on Victorian models, to be found in London's West End, in most of the major provincial theatres, at the Royal National Theatre in London or the Royal Shakespeare Theatre at Stratford-upon-Avon. If your experience of theatre-going is not very wide, think of a cinema: a flat wall with a (curtained) rectangular screen and the audience grouped in seats opposite to it; the screen is brightly illuminated, the auditorium in darkness. The shape of a cinema is based on the Victorian theatre or music-hall, with its rectangular picture-frame stage and proscenium arch, its stage lighting and darkened auditorium, and most of the audience (apart from the stage-boxes) sitting end-on to face the stage. Similar stages are often to be found in school halls, hospitals and other municipal buildings. Some theatres – such as the Royal Shakespeare Theatre at Stratford-upon-Avon – have the proscenium arch removed to create an 'open' stage: but the basic shape remains – the spectator looks through a rectangular frame at an illuminated spectacle.

The Elizabethan theatres were open-air buildings, whereas now we think of theatre as an interior event; the only lighting available to such a theatre was therefore natural daylight – so there could be no special effects of lighting, and the members of the audience could all see one another. Many members of the audience would be standing for the performance, in very close proximity to the stage – something we would expect as spectators at a football match, but not at a play. There was no pictorial scenery and there were no stage sets to localize the action in a particular place and time. The audience would be surrounding the stage on three, possibly four, sides in the manner of a theatre-in-the-round – so the actors had to play in three directions, and the separation between stage and audience which we regard as normal did not exist in the same degree.

The physical resources available to the players were thus basically very simple: a bare, flat stage, a small playing area above; and two doors for entrances and exits. The stage directions in the texts indicate how the physical architecture of the contemporary theatre would have been employed in performance. The two doors might have been used to suggest, for example, the simultaneous appearances of people coming from different places. Thus at II.i Portia and the Prince of Morocco, each accompanied by a train of followers, would have entered simultaneously from separate doors: '*Enter Morochus . . . and three or four followers accordingly, with Portia, Nerrissa and their traine*'. The gallery above the stage may have been used for musicians or for additional spectators. It was also required as an acting area 'above' at some points in some plays, but that does not necessarily exclude its occupation by either spectators or musicians. Most stage directions in Elizabethan texts prescribing action 'above' involve only one or two actors, and very little in the way of physical action, for the simple reason that any extensive or elaborate performance on this upper level would not have been clearly visible to all members of the audience. The stage directions in *The Merchant of Venice* call for action in this upper area of the stage only once – when in II.vi Jessica appears 'above', to signify that she is inside Shylock's house and therefore on a level above the street where Lorenzo and his companions stand. Jessica is required only to show herself briefly, and to speak a few lines from what may have been only a small aperture – signifying a window of Shylock's house – before disappearing, to make her way down through the tiring-house to re-emerge and join her lover, Lorenzo, on the main stage.

Much scholarly discussion of the staging of Elizabethan plays has been based on the assumption that the theatres had, in addition to the resources detailed above, an inner stage or 'discovery-space' at the back of the platform stage, recessed into the tiring-house, which could have been closed off from the main stage by curtains. Such an additional space would have provided an obvious opportunity for the staging of the casket scenes. Indeed the text seems to prescribe such an enclosed, additional space by its own internal stage directions:

> PORTIA   *Go, draw aside the curtains and discover*
>   *The several caskets to this noble Prince.*
>
>   (II.vii.1–2)

Now of course this direction does not require anything so elaborate as an 'inner stage', and was probably handled by the much simpler arrangement of a table with a screen or curtains concealing it from the audience until the moment of discovery. Since both the yard and galleries which held the audience seem to have stretched right around to the back of the platform stage, the actors could not have retired into an inner stage without disappearing from the view of at least some members of the audience. The same conditions which restricted the use of the balcony above the stage seem to me to make it improbable that there was such an inner stage, at least in the theatre where and when *The Merchant of Venice* was originally performed. Without such an inner stage, the casket scenes would have had to be acted on the main stage together with the rest of the drama. That pattern of staging would require a non-naturalistic method of performance, in which the curtained table would have been permanently visible but not always relevant: excluded from or brought into view, according to the requirements of the dramatic narrative. If a discovery-space was present and was employed in productions of this play, it could have been little more than a shallow recess holding the table with the caskets. The mysterious rituals of choice would still have occupied exactly the same dramatic territory as the Venetian street scenes. The curtains would have been a simple device of concealment for the caskets, not stage curtains fencing off a separate acting area. So the physical resources of the stage clearly worked in a symbolic, emblematic way rather than, like the stage technology of later theatres, aiming at a convincing realism of dramatic presentation.

The stage had no movable scenery, and no artificial lighting: the visual setting therefore remained virtually the same, except for the use of props, for every production, and for all the different parts of a single production, and the performances were lit by ordinary daylight. As the audience surrounded the stage, the action would be perceived from many different points of view, so the carefully calculated visual effects – designed to be perceived identically by all members of the audience – we are used to seeing in a modern theatre would not really be possible.

A further point to be aware of is that the acting companies of this period did not perform only in purpose-built theatres. There were still strong traditions of commissioned private entertainment whereby the actors would be paid to perform at court, in a hall of the nobility or at a citizen's house. The actors of Shakespeare's company might have played at their public playhouse in the afternoon, and repeated the performance in another place, where they would not be able to rely on the availability of theatrical devices, in the evening. Two performances of *The Merchant* are recorded as having taken place at the court of James I, in 1605. In addition, the companies continued to tour the provinces after they were established in their own purpose-built theatres, taking their productions to many different venues and locations. The actors must therefore have adopted the most flexible and opportunistic approach to their craft, always ready to improvise the performance in changed surroundings. They would not always have been able to rely even on having a stage level 'above' on which Jessica could appear for her elopement scene, or a curtained discovery-space with which to set the ritual of the caskets.

Time and Place

It almost goes without saying that the stage of the early modern public playhouse, at its most primitive and unfurnished (as represented in the familiar drawing of the Swan Theatre), must have been capable of providing the theatrical resources necessary for producing *The Merchant of Venice*, but only on condition that a certain approach to the drama was adopted. The theatre must have been largely or completely non-illusionistic, no attempt being considered necessary to make the stage look like a real place. Since the Elizabethan theatres used a bare stage without scenery, there was no representation of *place* as there often is in modern theatre productions, and as there almost invariably is in dramatic media such as television and film, which represent locations directly and unmistakably, by filming their physical equivalents – a city, a domestic interior, a forest, a sea-shore. In the Elizabethan theatre, this didn't really present a problem at all. Since the stage didn't represent any particular place, it could be imagined as representing any place necessary or convenient for the scene. Without any formal visual signifying of place, such as pictorial scenery or painted backdrops, the stage could not imitate place to establish location in the manner of later theatres, so time and place had to be signalled by convention, usually announced in the script itself.

Thus the scene known in modern editions of *The Merchant of Venice* as II.vi opens with Gratiano, who is waiting (we gather from the text) in the street outside Shylock's house to meet Lorenzo, saying 'This is the penthouse under which Lorenzo / Desired us to make stand'. The only clue the audience has as to the imagined whereabouts of the actors is what they say; it is then up to the audience to supply imaginatively the necessary context of location. This does not mean that every member of the Elizabethan audience immediately began to hallucinate the front of a Venetian usurer's house, but only that they would willingly enter into an agreement to consider the stage to be signifying, for the moment, that particular time and place: to realize, for example, that when Jessica appears on the gallery that she was to be understood as appearing at a window. In the Elizabethan theatre the stage was both everywhere and nowhere: it automatically became, in terms of location, whatever the actors claimed it was. In a modern production which identifies Shylock's house by constructing on stage a realistic set resembling a house-front, Gratiano's opening remark might seem unnecessary, but in the Elizabethan theatre, where the descriptive remark actually enables the audience without any visual prompting to identify the required location, it was a constitutive element of the drama.

Modern editions of Shakespeare's plays derive from texts developed by eighteenth-century scholars to 'modernize' the sixteenth and seventeenth-century printed texts that were already beginning to appear difficult and old-fashioned. These early editors naturally thought about the plays in performance in the context of their own type of theatre, which was already very different from the theatres in which Shakespeare's plays were originally produced. The original texts of *The Merchant of Venice* do not contain act and scene divisions since such divisions were not needed in the kind of theatre for which they were written. On a stage where there is no physical alteration between one scene and another, apart from the changing of dramatis personae, there is no such thing as a formal scene-change: all the text needs to prescribe is the movement of actors – who comes on, who goes off. The Elizabethan dramatic text was tailored for the Elizabethan dramatic space, where scenes were simply rapidly alternating episodes involving changing configurations and dispositions of actors.

By the time eighteenth-century editors were reshaping Shakespeare's plays into what they considered a more intelligible form of modern dramatic text, the contemporary stage was using pictorial scenery to 'set' a location in unmistakable visual terms. Location was established by the use of such scenery and maintained by frequent and elaborate scene changes. Hence eighteenth and nineteenth-century texts prescribe different locations, and imply theatrical scene changes, within their construction of the dramatic narrative. All current modern editions retain the act and scene divisions introduced by eighteenth-century editors, though often in square brackets to indicate that they were not present in the original text. Some, like the Arden Shakespeare, also retain the indicators of location which were anachronistically interpolated by eighteenth-century scholars to make the Elizabethan text fit into the production system of the contemporary theatre: thus in the Arden text of *The Merchant of Venice*, scenes are identified as taking place in 'Venice' or 'Belmont', or occasionally with more specificity, as for the trial scene – 'Venice. A Court of Justice', or for the concluding scene – 'Belmont. A Grove or Green Place before Portia's House'. It was clearly intended, from the conversation that takes place in the final scene, that the actors should be imagined as occupying a garden or other space outside Portia's house, and that their final exit through the stage doors should have been understood as an entrance into the house itself. But the 'Grove or Green Place' is a memory of eighteenth and nineteenth-century productions (the cover illustration of this book is derived from exactly such a memory) and was never seen on Shakespeare's stage.

The much admired descriptive poetry, that brings imaginatively alive that romantic night of bright moonlight and sweet winds in Act V, was originally uttered on a completely bare stage during an open-air afternoon performance on the south bank of the River Thames. The poetry was there to create the illusion of darkness and romance, not to serve as an otiose repetition of an already established visual effect. When Portia enters and observes the light burning in her hall, she would in such a performance have done so in broad daylight. Darkness could never be made visible as in a modern theatre, so a night scene would have to be defined by dialogue – 'The moon shines bright' (v.i.1) – or by a combination of gestures and props – such as the burning of candles or torches – 'That light we see is burning in my hall' (v.i.89). But these were all the 'special effects' needed for the lively imaginations of the Elizabethan audience to convert sober daylight into romantic night. In an original production the actor would thus have used one of those special effects as a cue for Portia's surprisingly melancholy reflections on her own recent success. That gesture was obviously typical of the extraordinary economy of the Elizabethan stage, where a paucity of theatrical resources seems to have co-existed with an immensely fertile and creative dramatic imagination.

Inside and Out

In their efforts to rationalize the Shakespearean text, eighteenth-century editors frequently created unnecessary confusion by their failure to understand the play in its original theatrical context. It is not at all clear whether some of the scenes set in Venice – for example, the opening scene of the play – are imagined as taking place inside a house, or in some public place such as a street or piazza. The point is that it simply does not matter one way or the other: the 'place' of the action is merely a focal point where the characters can meet, cross, pass or encounter one another so as to form a dramatic action. In the Belmont scenes, things are quite different: the casket scenes, which constitute most of the Belmont action, are clearly set in an interior location, and reinforce the strong sense in Belmont of a house, a home, a space of settlement and family continuity. Some of the Venice scenes are clearly set in public places (II.ii, II.iv, II.vi, III.i, III.iii, IV.ii) and it is possible that all the Venice scenes, with the obvious exception of the trial scene (IV.i), are intended as taking place outside rather than in. Certainly none of the scenes involving the Christian characters appears to take place within an interior or private space that can be thought of as their home. In one sense they enjoy the freedom of the city, being as much at home in those open public spaces as in any private domestic dwelling. In another sense they belong nowhere, and the absence of privacy can be thought of as accentuating that odd sense of alienation I have already noted as characterizing the life of the Venetian Christians. Certainly Belmont, which the Christians ultimately occupy, has a much stronger sense of private space than anything apparently afforded by the city of Venice.

But there is at least one Venetian who definitely occupies a private domestic space, and that is Shylock. II.v is a scene which obviously takes place inside Shylock's house. In this scene Shylock harangues Launcelot and shouts for Jessica, speaks indiscreetly about his relationship with the Christians and vents his anger against Christian festivity; every element of the action suggests that he is inside a private space, safely able to voice his true opinions of the dominant culture. Yet eighteenth-century editors placed this scene in the street – the Arden edition preserves Edmund Malone's stage direction 'Venice. Before Shylock's House'. Their reason for doing so is simply that this scene is followed immediately by the scene in which Lorenzo meets the other Christians outside Shylock's house, and abducts Jessica. The normal definition of a scene change – that all the characters in the previous scene leave the stage – is there to separate II.v from II.vi, yet the eighteenth-century editors obviously felt that the scenes were so close together as to suggest a possible consistency of location. If the previous scene could also be located outside Shylock's house, then the same place could be imagined as the setting for both II.v. and II.vi.

For an audience watching an original performance of *The Merchant of Venice* in an Elizabethan theatre, this juxtaposition of scenes would not have presented any problem at all. They would have been entirely happy to imagine the first scene as taking place inside Shylock's house and to assume that the exit of one set of actors (Shylock, Jessica, Launcelot) followed by the appearance of another set (Gratiano, Salerio, Lorenzo) was a shift sufficient to indicate a change of location from the inside of the house to the outside. Both Shylock's attempt to colonize and safeguard his own domestic space (by controlling his daughter and locking up his house) and the easy penetration of those defences by the Christian conspirators (who walk away with both daughter and ducats) are designed to take place in the same physical arena, the bare stage of the Elizabethan public playhouse.

Reality and Illusion

Obviously this kind of theatre made little or no attempt to create the illusion of realism on the stage. In many ways the Elizabethan stage was anti-illusionistic. For example, plays were probably constructed with a specific number of actors in mind, and characters were included or excluded from a scene according to the number of players available. Obviously if you see the same actor playing more than one part, it breaks down any illusion that the actor 'is' the character; rather the historical characters were 'impersonated' by actors who remained obviously, and all the time, actors. Launcelot Gobbo is referred to indiscriminately in the early texts personally by name and generically as 'Clowne': his role would have been partly located into the play as part of the action, and partly composed of ad-libbing and by-play with the audience, during which he would have appeared as comedian (clown) rather than character. The very slight share of the text given to Gobbo probably distorts the size of his role in the play: he would have been played by the company's resident comedian, and his role would have been largely extra-textual. Above all, the roles of women were played by boy actors and instead of seeking to hide this obvious anomaly, the plays are full of plots involving disguise and cross-dressing – like the disguising of Portia and Nerissa as Dr Balthasar and his clerk – which formally brought to the audience's attention an overt awareness of sexual difference.

The kind of archaeologically reconstructed historical costume we see in many modern performances did not appear on the Elizabethan stage. The theatres did not use historical costume at all – this did not become normal in theatres until the nineteenth century – but something closer to what we call modern dress – the ordinary costume of the time, embellished with conventional signs to indicate historical or geographical setting. Thus the stage direction indicating the entrance of the Prince of Morocco stipulates an exotic style of dress: *'Enter Morochus a tawnie Moore all in white'*. The physical objects required by plays of this period suggest a basic physical vocabulary of major props – a chair, a throne, a bed – which must either have remained on stage throughout, perhaps changing their uses according to the needs of the action, or which were carried on and off in full view of the audience. The text of *The Merchant of Venice* calls for hardly any props: a basket for Old Gobbo, masquing costume for the masque that fails to take place, letters, the three caskets and rings for the final scene.

All this need not mean that Elizabethan audiences watched their plays in intellectual detachment, always aware of the fictionality of the drama, never taken in by the historical illusion. On the contrary, a performance in an Elizabethan theatre was probably more exciting and involving than those of many modern theatres. The theatres were, by modern standards, very small (the recent discovery of the foundations of the Rose Theatre in Southwark brings this point forcibly home), and the audience tightly packed around the stage. No member of the audience would have been at any great distance from the stage or the action; there were no physical divisions, as there were in later theatres (proscenium arch, orchestra pit, footlights) to cut the audience off from the action.

A consideration of the original playing space also has profound implications for interpretation of the dramatic text. Although the Elizabethan drama was, as we have seen from our exploration of only one play, an extremely diversified and heterogeneous medium, its basic physical production space prescribed a certain overall unity, in the sense that the stage looked much the same for all plays and for the whole of any one play. Later productions of *The Merchant of Venice* began to use the technical resources of the modern theatre – stage lighting, scenery and sets, historical costume – to create a very obvious visual distinction between Venice and Belmont. The realistic commercial city and the romantic country estate would be represented as entirely different worlds, suffused with a radically different emotional atmosphere. Yet that distinction is, as our discussion has shown, actually very misleading, since Venice and Belmont are separate territories of the same social country; the Venetian Christians should be seen as in some ways essentially unified, rather than presented in radically discontinuous dimensions, sharply separated and distinguished one from another by stage technology. The kind of staging needed to produce an effect of sameness-with-difference – where distinctions can be made and then collapsed or withdrawn, and where dramatic contrasts can in the course of the action prove to be merely different facets of the same reality – was precisely that bare, flexible Elizabethan popular stage, which could pose a radical distinction through its dramatic language, only to reverse it a moment later. Peter Brook described the Elizabethan theatre as exactly such a space for the interaction of unreconciled contradictions:[2]

Shakespeare's plays were written to be performed continuously ... their cinematic structure of alternating short scenes, plot intercut with subplot, were all part of a total shape. This shape is only revealed dynamically, that is, in the uninterrupted sequence of these scenes, and without this their effect and power are lessened as much as would be a film that was projected with breaks and musical interludes between each reel.

The Elizabethan stage was ... a neutral open platform – just a place with some doors – and so it enabled the dramatist effortlessly to whip the spectator through an unlimited succession of illusions, covering, if he chose, the entire physical world.

These characteristics of the Shakespearean drama, obviously crucial to our understanding of *The Merchant of Venice*, only appear when we examine the play in its original textual form, and relocate it dramatically back into its original performance space on that 'neutral open platform' of the Elizabethan public stage.

6. Endgames

People often express a preference for happy rather than unhappy endings. Such a preference is often coupled with a wry acknowledgement that happy endings to novels or dramatic comedies are not realistic, that they belong to a realm of fantasy, in which the suffering, the misery, the intractable difficulties of 'real life' are temporarily banished or smoothed over. Happy endings in the theatre compensate us, perhaps, for the obvious and familiar fact that the 'stories' of people's lives do not always turn out so cheerfully. In a more sober and resigned frame of mind we may admit that tragedy provides a more accurate assessment of the chances of life, a more realistic acceptance of its ultimate outcomes. One way of telling the 'story' of Shakespeare's life as a dramatist is to propose that he favoured the genre of comedy when possessed by a spirit of optimism, and veered towards tragedy as his outlook on life clouded, saddened and matured.

Endings

Since all life ends with death, tragedy may be regarded as a true and accurate reflection of the nature of 'ending'. All life doesn't 'end' with marriage and reconciliation and forgiveness, as dramatic comedies do. But then life doesn't 'end' in any way at all, never comes to a stop, except with death. There is something paradoxical, then, about the two elements of the term 'happy ending'. Surely happiness is something we associate with stability, continuity, the assurance of unalloyed pleasure; if it comes to an 'ending', then we are being delivered over to the arbitrary diversity of real life, with its characteristic mixture of pleasures and pains.

It has often been suggested that the experience of reading or watching Shakespearean comedy is analogous to experiences of revelry, celebration, carnival – as if attending the play is like being at a party. If that is the case, then the prospect of the play's *ending* can only be regarded with regret, sadness, with the restlessness of unfulfilled desire. Watching a comedy in a theatre, we can temporarily inhabit, for the duration of the play, a world in which people can experience adventure without coming to harm, take risks with a guarantee of ultimate luck and turn themselves and their world upside-down with an assurance that things will always right themselves. For a permitted space we imaginatively occupy a world full of pleasure, liberty, fun and harmless excitement. When it comes to an end, however happily, we are turned out of the theatre into a real world where such purity of pleasure has no independent existence: a world where it rains, where the bus we are waiting for doesn't come, where loss and separation and denial are as much a part of life as love and fooling and celebration. Shakespearean characters often compare the situation of the play to the kind of pleasant dream from which awakening is a matter of regret. In *The Tempest* Caliban speaks of such dreams, visions of a haunting beauty that makes waking an experience of loss: 'when I woke, I cried to dream again.' Here a beginning (waking to reality) is also an ending (of the dream). A happy ending may thus entail the ending of happiness.

Harmony and Discord

The Merchant of Venice ends with restoration, reconciliation and unity. Misunderstandings are cleared up and identities restored. Shylock has been defeated, and Antonio saved from the murderous power of his enmity. All the characters return to Belmont from Venice: Bassanio and Gratiano to occupy their newly colonized territory, Portia and Nerissa to enter their new status as wives. Identity is restored, as Portia and Nerissa reveal their strategy of impersonation, and turn their assumed masculine disguise inside out to reveal their true feminine selves. The members of the cast are largely organized into heterosexual couples (Bassanio/Portia, Gratiano/Nerissa, Lorenzo/Jessica), so the convention of marriage is employed to align the characters into an orderly configuration. The comedy closes in the moonlit tranquillity of Portia's (or rather now Bassanio's) garden, with social integration and unity.

Thus *The Merchant of Venice* appears by this ending to be shaped into a dominant pattern of ultimate reconciliation, harmonized, unified, balanced. The comic pattern concludes by reconciling all contradictions, resolving all disharmonies, drawing all discordant elements into a unitary synthesis and integration. At the end of the play, this pattern is effected by various dramatic and poetic means: the symbolic harmony of marriage; the reconciliation of disagreement (the dispute over the rings is a practical joke, a staged quarrel deliberately faked so as to restore subsequent unanimity); the clarification of deception and misunderstanding, especially the throwing off of disguise; and the symbolic harmony of music, familiarly acknowledged as the physical embodiment, in Elizabethan drama, of psychological and social concord.

Lorenzo's set piece speech on the music of the spheres unites all these
levels of concord into a complex but unitary synthesis:

LORENZO   *My friend Stephano, signify, I pray you,*
          Within the house, your mistress is at hand,
          And bring your music forth into the air.

Exit Stephano

          How sweet the moonlight sleeps upon this bank!
          Here will we sit and let the sounds of music
          Creep in our ears; soft stillness and the night
          Become the touches of sweet harmony.
          Sit, Jessica. Look how the floor of heaven
          Is thick inlaid with patens of bright gold.
          There's not the smallest orb which thou beholdest
          But in his motion like an angel sings,
          Still quiring to the young-eyed cherubins;
          Such harmony is in immortal souls,
          But whilst this muddy vesture of decay
          Doth grossly close it in, we cannot hear it.

Enter Musicians

          Come ho, and wake Diana with a hymn,
          With sweetest touches pierce your mistress' ear
          And draw her home with music.

Music
(V.i.51–68)

The speech formally links the idea of harmony in music with its physical
demonstration (*Music plays*), the peaceful harmony of nature with the
unanimity of achieved relationship, the integrity of the soul with the
elemental music of the spheres (a revised edition of the Folio text
intensified this emphasis on harmony by correcting 'patens' – the small
gold dishes used in church communion services – to 'patterns'). The
musicians herald the return of Portia, whose successfully achieved quest
prefigures unity and reconciliation among the play's dominant Christian
community.

How perfect in fact is this harmony? Are there no jarring notes, no
false strings? Does the comic pattern succeed in governing into integration all the discordant elements it strives to contain? Or are there
elements in the play which resist integration, defy reconciliation, refuse
to be synthesized into the general comic perspective? To propose a
suggestive comparison, *Twelfth Night* is known as one of the most
serene and beautiful of Shakespeare's comedies, but as that play draws

to its resolution, a shadow is cast across its theatrical concordat by the rejection of Malvolio. Like Shylock, Malvolio is perhaps a man more sinning than sinned against, but the play allows us at least the possibility of regarding him as a victim of persecution. He is a fool, but is he less ridiculous than the fashionably melancholy egotist, Orsino? Is it natural justice that self-absorbed folly in a Duke should reap such rich reward, while narcissistic blindness in a steward deserves ridicule and humiliation? Olivia certainly agrees that Malvolio has been 'notoriously abus'd'. In the conclusion to *Twelfth Night* we are aware that the harmonizing and reconciliation of contradictions exact a certain price: that someone has to suffer by exclusion from what would otherwise be a perfect unity. Malvolio's exit casts a shadow over the play's conclusion.

It would be wrong to over-emphasize this detail. But it must at least force the possibility of glimpsing an alternative to the harmonious and optimistic perspective of the dominant group of characters, and that is another point of view: that of the alienated and excluded outsider. For Malvolio, as for Shylock, the comic ending is tragic. If we refuse to accept the validity of that perspective, if we dissociate our emotions from the tragedies of Malvolio and Shylock, then while we are accepting the comic pattern as dominant, we are surely declining to hear a particularly poignant strain in the play's poetic music. At the end of *Twelfth Night* we watch Malvolio rushing off-stage, shouting his absurd threat of vengeance ('I'll be revenged on the whole pack of you!'), and respond with a laughter which, though not uncompromised by guilt and anxiety, depends on a commitment to the comic reconciliation of the Illyrian court. In another play by Shakespeare we witness the spectacle of an old man who has acted foolishly, who has also suffered from the curse of self-love, rushing out into a storm, shouting a very similar imprecation of revenge, wrung from the agony of impotence: 'I will do such things . . .'. There in *King Lear* the perspective is unmistakably tragic, only because the dramatic structure inclines us to view the situation from the point of view of the excluded, rather than from the perspective of those who, for whatever reasons, exclude.

This is not an attempt to revalue *Twelfth Night* as a tragedy: it is rather to insist on the tragic potentiality of some of its elements. We don't take Malvolio's revenge seriously, because we are assured of the benevolent and beneficial power of the harmonized court. The closer we draw to Malvolio's own situation, the clearer our perception of him as a victim of persecution, the more understandable becomes his demand for revenge. Which brings us back to Shylock. Both Malvolio and Shylock are members of a minority group within their respective

societies: a Puritan and a Jew. In history such minorities have been
cruelly persecuted and oppressed, but each too has had its moments of
triumph or acceptance. Malvolio's revenge on the carefree and irresponsible aristocracy took concrete form not long after Shakespeare's death,
with the Civil War and the execution of a king. In 1655 Oliver Cromwell,
leader of the organized Malvolios, re-admitted the Jews to England for
the first time since their banishment in 1209. As commercial production
and exchange became in the course of England's 'bourgeois revolution'
more dependent on a money economy, requiring the free flow of credit
and finance, Puritan and Jew found themselves in economic partnership,
and Malvolio found in Shylock an indispensable ally.

There are of course much stronger grounds for attempting to view
The Merchant of Venice from the point of view of its defeated 'villain',
who throws a much longer and darker shadow, both within and beyond
the play, than that which Malvolio casts over the ending of *Twelfth
Night*. There are, however, disharmonies other than the repressed
memory of Shylock reverberating within this final scene. Another
shadow, albeit a considerably smaller one, is cast by the presence of
Antonio. Antonio is after all, nominally at least, the central character
of the play, the merchant of the title, and we would expect him therefore
to be prominent in the dramatic ritual of celebration that closes the
play. Antonio, however, appears marginalized in comparison with the
other characters, all of whom have a much more definite role to play.
He merely shadows Bassanio when husband and wife formally greet
one another, and inexplicably utters no word of greeting or salutation:

> BASSANIO   *... Give welcome to my friend,*
> *This is the man, this is Antonio,*
> *To whom I am so infinitely bound.*
> PORTIA   *You should in all sense be much bound to him,*
> *For, as I hear, he was much bound for you.*
>
>   (V.i.133–7)

Portia addresses Antonio obliquely, with a remark that can be read as
another indirect barb of irony against Bassanio, connecting with her
remark at the end of III.ii: 'Since you are dear bought, I will love you
dear.' Portia points out that while her husband expresses a general
indebtedness to Antonio, being 'bound' (meaning 'obliged') to him, it
was Antonio who was much more seriously bound (by the flesh-bond)
in Shylock's contract. Antonio's response is not a reply to Portia's
greeting, but a defence of his friend, and even then it consists of only
one line:

> ANTONIO   *No more than I am well acquitted of.*
>
> (V.i.138)

Portia's reply is abrupt, almost churlish:

> PORTIA   *Sir, you are very welcome to our house;*
> *It must appear in other ways than words,*
> *Therefore I scant this breathing courtesy.*
>
> (V.i.139–41)

Antonio then remains silent, further marginalized by the quarrel over the rings, that impromptu dramatization of domestic conflict from which he is pointedly excluded by his bachelor status. The quarrel is also a matter of embarrassment to him, since it is in one sense of his making:

> ANTONIO   *I am th'unhappy subject of these quarrels.*
>
> (V.i.238)

It could obviously be argued that too much can be made of these details. Antonio, we could say, is clearly welcomed into the integrated harmony of Belmont, as Bassanio's friend and as the living trophy of Portia's courtroom victory. Portia's tone is not indicative of genuine discourtesy, but deliberately assumed to arouse and puzzle the new-comers – a kind of 'warm-up' for the full-scale mock quarrel that follows. Antonio's true welcome, accompanied by an unexpected free gift, comes in the course of Portia's speech of revelation in which the full story of the trial is disclosed:

> PORTIA   . . . *Antonio, you are welcome,*
> *And I have better news in store for you ·*
> *Than you expect. Unseal this letter soon,*
> *There you shall find three of your argosies*
> *Are richly come to harbour suddenly.*
>
> (V.i.273–7)

Nothing surely could contrast more sharply than the respective fates of Shylock and Antonio: the one defeated, rejected and his wealth expropriated; the other redeemed, welcomed and rewarded with unlooked-for good fortune. But the very means by which Portia reveals this upturn in Antonio's fortune seems to me to marginalize him even further. Antonio moves from being a shadowy figure at Bassanio's side, to becoming the embarrassed witness of a marital quarrel, and finally, through Portia's machinations is made the grateful recipient of aristocratic bounty. It is worth observing that Lorenzo gets his present at the same time and in the same form as Antonio, as if the gifts are parallel rituals of charity.

> NERISSA *There do I give to you and Jessica*
> *From the rich Jew, a special deed of gift,*
> *After his death, of all he dies possessed of.*
> (V.i.291–3)

Yet nothing could be more different than the situations of the two characters in question. Antonio has risked death for Portia's husband, and is expected to be grateful to receive not even a gift, but the return of some of his own property. Lorenzo has suffered nothing worse than the strain of helping Jessica to carry off her father's wealth and yet is rewarded with the substantial wealth acquired for him at Antonio's request, but here distributed as largesse from Portia's bounty.

Finally, there is the striking exclusion of Antonio from the otherwise ubiquitous marital pairings which organize the rest of the cast into couples. The conventions of romantic comedy could easily have been used arbitrarily to find Antonio a wife (surely Portia might have had an identical twin sister, hitherto for mysterious reasons disguised as a servant?), but for some reason Antonio is left wifeless. This uncomfortable fact can be disguised in performance, but it remains an obvious anomaly. As the various wedded couples enter Belmont to consummate their marriages, what exactly is Antonio going to do? Sleep on his own? Wriggle in between Bassanio and Portia? Even the simple physical mechanics of getting the characters off-stage can present problems where one of them is so pointedly left out of the otherwise universal heterosexual coupling: should Antonio be escorted off between Bassanio and Portia? Should he follow after them? Should he tag along behind, after all the other characters have exited? Clearly the play has not succeeded in integrating Antonio sufficiently into the 'universal' celebration of harmony for these questions to be readily answered. As Bassanio's devoted friend, perhaps he will find a place of affection between husband and wife. As Bassanio's thwarted homosexual lover, perhaps he won't. The acidity of Portia's attitude towards Antonio may be part of the prank she and Nerissa are playing; or it may be a reaction to the inconvenience of a *ménage-à-trois*.

To the very end then, Shylock and Antonio, the Jew and the Merchant of the play's interchangeable titles, remain connected to one another in a destiny deeper than the comic resolution of the play.[1] Antonio remains as firmly de-centred from the final resolution as he was from the initial romantic action: a bystander, a witness, even in some senses a victim. This marginalization of the central character can be viewed in the theoretical contexts of sexuality and of economics. In sexual terms, Antonio is literally the odd man out, the lone homosexual who is never wholly integrated even into the communities to which he most obviously belongs.[2] In economic terms, Antonio the trader stands outside the significant socio-economic alliance, which is that between the impoverished gentry (Bassanio) and the landed aristocracy (Portia). The merchant is regarded as a useful, but by no means an indispensable, adjunct to that alliance.

We can begin to see now how remarkably interesting this play is to modern theoretical criticism with its specific concerns with matters of race and sexuality. Both Jew and homosexual merchant are identified in terms of cultural difference, and though their fates are very different – one excluded, the other tolerated – neither has the benefit of full participation in the social life of the community. Perhaps even more surprisingly, the play also offers some significant hints to the effect that another minority within the play finds itself less than wholly satisfied by the comic denouement – the women.

When Bassanio has chosen the correct casket, Portia, in a highly formal speech of dedication and submission, gives herself over to Bassanio, renouncing her authority as lord of Belmont and subjecting her personality entirely to that of her husband.

> PORTIA *You see me, Lord Bassanio, where I stand,*
> *Such as I am . . .*
> *. . . an unlessoned girl, unschooled, unpractisèd,*
> *Happy in this, she is not yet so old*
> *But she may learn . . .*
> *Happiest of all is that her gentle spirit*
> *Commits itself to yours to be directed,*
> *As from her lord, her governor, her king.*
> *Myself and what is mine to you and yours*
> *Is now converted. But now I was the lord*
> *Of this fair mansion, master of my servants,*
> *Queen o'er myself; and even now, but now,*
> *This house, these servants, and this same myself*
> *Are yours, my lord's. I give them with this ring . . .*
>   (III.ii.149–50, 159–61, 163–71)

If we return to the distinction I made in my Introduction between traditional historicist and post-structuralist readings, we will find the different theoretical approaches producing very different readings of this speech. The traditional historicist reading, committed to understanding the language of the speech in the context of Elizabethan ideas and beliefs, would argue that Portia is voicing the orthodox views of her age on marriage, in which the woman voluntarily surrendered her body, property and possessions to her masculine superior. A post-structuralist reading would argue that the modern reader cannot, or at least should not, read this speech without the informing context of modern feminist thought. If Portia means what she says, then she stands in this perspective as a sad example of female subjection. Either she is unconscious of this self-abnegation, or fully aware of it, but resigned to accept it. Clearly the speech could be spoken either as a rapt and enthusiastic speech of self-committal, or a melancholy lament for the power and privilege she is losing and now must surrender to Bassanio. If she does not mean it – and one line of the speech ('As from her lord, her governor, her king') appears word for word the same as a line from a speech in *The Taming of the Shrew* in which, by general agreement, the woman cannot possibly be saying what she means – then the speech is either part of a comic routine or part of a complex structure of irony.

We have already seen from our discussion of III.iv that the play gives its own unequivocal answer to this question by allowing Portia to subvert the spirit of this speech by her own immediate actions. In III.iv she announces her intention of assuming a masculine disguise, and following Bassanio to Venice, equipped with a much more formidable plan of campaign than any she confided in her husband. The persistent irony, as I noted above, is that the women have to disguise themselves as men in order to acquire the freedom necessary to compensate for the weaknesses and shortcomings of the men themselves. Portia signals this strongly by making fun of masculine pretensions. Their husbands will see them again, sooner than they imagine.

> PORTIA   ... *but in such a habit*
> *That they shall think we are accomplishèd*
> *With that we lack ...*
>   *... I have within my mind*
> *A thousand raw tricks of these bragging Jacks,*
> *Which I will practise.*
>
>   (III.iv.60–62, 76–8)

Once disguised as men, their husbands will assume them to be possessed of male genitals, precisely the thing they 'lack'. It was common in this period to think of the female body as incomplete, and of the female genitalia as 'lacking' something – the penis. If women had 'no thing'

73

(no penis), then they obviously had 'nothing'. Such an assumption belongs to an ideology of masculine domination, in which positive force is invested in the male phallus, and the female is identified as phallically deficient and therefore inferior, the weaker sex. At the same time, however, Portia uses her scathing female wit to satirize men and their pretensions: a woman must, to disguise herself as a man, accomplish a sustained exercise in merciless parody of the vanity and immaturity of men.

In the trial scene, Portia proves herself to be 'lacking' in nothing: to be, indeed, infinitely superior in resourcefulness, intelligence, knowledge and determination to any of the men in question, including her husband. By means of that masculine disguise she is able to reassume some of the power she has relinquished by surrendering her lordship of Belmont to Bassanio. On her return to Belmont, however, she must put off both her disguise and her pretensions to continuing power: Bassanio is the master now. As she approaches her former property, Portia seems suddenly possessed of a deep strain of melancholy, a plangent sense of unappeasable loss:

> PORTIA *That light we see is burning in my hall;*
> *How far that little candle throws his beams!*
> *So shines a good deed in a naughty world.*
> (V.i.89–91)

Still thinking of Belmont as her own house (a phrase which is presently adjusted to 'our house', 139), Portia appropriates the candle as a symbol of her own recent action in redeeming Antonio from her husband's debt: she too is the 'little candle' (we remember her opening words, 'My little body is aweary of this great world' (I.ii.1–2) which shines brightly but alone in an otherwise unrelieved darkness of wickedness and futility. In view of Portia's astounding success, the observation is a surprisingly modest celebration of her achievement. Perhaps it is the weight of responsibility, which, like her initial world-weariness, would be unintelligible to anyone observing her circumstances from the outside. Or perhaps Portia is simply overwhelmed, as she returns from a scene of triumphant action to find her house occupied by others, by an inconsolable sense of loss. Nerissa's speech sounds the same melancholy note:

> NERISSA *When the moon shone we did not see the candle.*
> PORTIA *So doth the greater glory dim the less.*
> *A substitute shines brightly as a king*
> *Until a king be by, and then his state*

> *Empties itself, as doth an inland brook*
> *Into the main of waters.*
>
> (V.i.92–7)

Portia's entry into the state of marriage is anticipated as an eclipsing of her powers by the 'king' ('lord' and 'governor') to whom she has entrusted and committed herself and her previous status. As soon as the 'king' arrives, on Bassanio's return, her petty brightness will fade into insignificance, her authority will 'empty itself' as a stream disappears into the sea. Even more discordant than the victimization of Shylock and the marginalization of Antonio is this melancholy voice of female subjection. Certainly for Portia this is an 'ending', though it scarcely purports to be a happy one.

On the other hand, a more positive feminist reading of the text might note this sense of subjection, but draw attention also to the fact that Portia signifies her surrender of power to Bassanio by the giving of the ring which he subsequently bestows on 'Dr Balthasar'. The dispute over the rings is of course comic, since Dr Balthasar is only Portia in disguise, and Bassanio is actually returning the ring to his own wife. But symbolically the dispute over the rings may be understood to have its more serious side, as if Portia is claiming that Bassanio's having been tricked into surrendering the ring invalidates her original act of renunciation. It is indisputable that the faked quarrel in V.i, followed by Portia's various revelations and her distributing of gifts, places her in a position of unmistakable dominance. The actress playing Portia has ample opportunity to suggest that, despite her meek submission to her new lord, Portia is determined not to surrender the reins of power she has been accustomed to exercise. Perhaps it is ultimately Bassanio's very weakness of character that makes him the right choice of suitor for the imperious heiress of Belmont.

I have ended this essay as I began, with a focus on *The Merchant of Venice* interpreted in the light of modern theoretical concerns with issues of race and sexuality. Where more traditional readings would address that final scene entirely in terms of a dramatic and social model of harmony and reconciliation, I have dwelt on the way in which that harmony is undermined by exclusion or marginalization of the three characters who represent what we might now call subjugated cultural minorities – the Jewish moneylender, the homosexual merchant, the married woman. It is in its address to such social, cultural, political, economic, sexual and ideological problems that a text like this has something to say to the world in which it is read. But to return to the

question initially posed in the Introduction: is such a theoretically informed critical reading appropriately addressed to the formal and historical nature of the play, or is it rather an attempt to measure the play by
values of which its author could have had no knowledge? I have tried
to read *The Merchant of Venice* by an act of historical imagination, as a
document of its time, and by the application of a modern theoretical
consciousness, as a text of our own time. Can we ever at any point be
entirely sure, when engaged in such a dialectical process of reading,
whether a particular act of interpretation or effort of understanding is a
historical or a contemporary phenomenon? Am I seeing in the play
potentialities which its first spectators could also have seen? Or am I
reading into the play modern concerns of which the play itself could
have had no prior knowledge? My own belief is that these different
perspectives are inseparable elements of a single process: that our
present-day concerns find echoes in these old texts, and are in turn
informed and modified by the authentic historical difference of the old
texts themselves. But these questions are ultimately for readers to
answer, in the process of their own critical and theoretical explorations
both of texts and of the activity of theoretical criticism.

Notes

Introduction

1. Walter Cohen, 'The Merchant of Venice and the Possibilities of Historical Criticism', *ELH*, 1982, XLIX:iv, p. 767.
2. W. H. Auden, 'Brothers and Others' from *The Dyer's Hand*, 1963, quoted from *Shakespeare's Comedies: An Anthology of Modern Criticism*, ed. Laurence Lerner, Penguin, 1967, p. 143.
3. Graham Midgely, 'The Merchant of Venice: A Reconsideration' from *Essays in Criticism*, 1960, X, p. 121.
4. Heinrich Heine, from 'Shakespeares Mädchen und Frauen', 1839, quoted from 'The Merchant of Venice': A Selection of Critical Essays, ed. John Wilders, Macmillan, 1969, p. 29.
5. See E. M. W. Tillyard, *Shakespeare's Problem Plays*, Chatto and Windus, 1950.
6. Giovanni Fiorentino, *Il Pecorone*, written in the late fourteenth century, published in 1558. See *The Merchant of Venice*, ed. W. Moelwyn Merchant, Penguin, 1967, pp. 18–19; and *The Merchant of Venice*, ed. John Russell Brown, Methuen, 1955, pp. xxviii–xxx.
7. The term was coined by Stephen Greenblatt, whose *Shakespearean Negotiations*, Oxford University Press, 1988, exemplifies the method. See also, for a consideration of Judaism in Renaissance drama, his essay 'Marlowe, Marx and Anti-Semitism' in Stephen Greenblatt, *Learning to Curse*, Routledge, 1990.
8. William Hazlitt, quoted by John Russell Brown in *The Merchant of Venice*, Methuen, p. xxxiv.
9. Henry Irving, quoted by John Russell Brown in *The Merchant of Venice*, Methuen, pp. xxxiv–xxxv.
10. Irving's production reviewed in *Blackwood's Magazine*, December 1879, p. 655.
11. William Poel, quoted in *The Merchant of Venice*, ed. M. M. Mahood, Cambridge University Press, 1987, p. 48.

1. Venice and Belmont

1. See Harold C. Goddard, 'The Three Caskets' from *The Meaning of*

    Shakespeare, 1963, extracted from *'The Merchant of Venice': A Selection of Critical Essays*, ed. John Wilders, Macmillan, 1969.

2. Luke 15:11–32. The play does not, on the other hand, dwell on the parable of the talents – Matthew 25:14–31.
3. W. H. Auden, 'Brothers and Others' from *The Dyer's Hand*, 1963, quoted from *Shakespeare's Comedies: An Anthology of Modern Criticism*, ed. Laurence Lerner, Penguin, 1967, p. 153.

2. Economics and Sexuality

1. See John Palmer, 'Shylock' from *Comic Characters of Shakespeare*, 1946, extracted from *'The Merchant of Venice': A Selection of Critical Essays*, ed. John Wilders, Macmillan, 1969.
2. See Walter Cohen, '*The Merchant of Venice* and the Possibilities of Historical Criticism', *ELH*, 1982, XLIX:iv, p. 769.
3. See Cohen, 1982, p. 772: 'The concluding tripartite unity of Antonio, Bassanio and Portia enacts precisely this interclass harmony between aristocratic landed wealth and mercantile capital, with the former dominant'. See also E. C. Pettet, '*The Merchant of Venice* and the Problem of Usury' in *'The Merchant of Venice': A Selection of Critical Essays*, ed. John Wilders, Macmillan, 1969.

3. Jews and Christians

1. See *The Merchant of Venice*, ed. M. M. Mahood, Cambridge University Press, 1987, pp. 48–50.
2. See Harold C. Goddard, 'The Three Caskets' from *The Meaning of Shakespeare*, 1963, extracted from *'The Merchant of Venice': A Selection of Critical Essays*, ed. John Wilders, Macmillan, 1969.

4. Law and Power

1. The Prince of Morocco trusts that Portia will not display racial prejudice in acknowledging him as a suitor: 'Mislike me not for my complexion' (II.i.1). Portia, however, displays exactly such prejudice as she breathes a sigh of relief at the outcome: 'Let all of his complexion choose me so' (II.vii.79).
2. Alexander Pope, in his edition of the play, relegated this line to a footnote, considering it unworthy of Shakespeare. But see *The Merchant of Venice*, ed. John Russell Brown, Methuen, 1955, p. lvii: 'Portia's assertion . . . is no longer a cold calculation, but a joyful acknowledgement of the pleasures of giving for love.'

5. The Elizabethan Stage

1. Some of these original texts, including a reprint of the first (1600) edition of *The Merchant of Venice*, as published in the first 'complete works' of Shakespeare, the First Folio of 1623, can be consulted in facsimile form in *The Norton Facsimile: The First Folio of Shakespeare*, ed. Charlton Hinman, Paul Hamlyn, 1968. Easily available editions of the original texts, unmediated by editorial interference, do not as yet exist, but such texts are being produced in the series *Shakespearean Originals*, edited by Graham Holderness and Bryan Loughrey, and published by Harvester Wheatsheaf.
2. Peter Brook, *The Empty Space*, Penguin, 1972, pp. 96–7.

6. Endgames

1. See Graham Midgely, '*The Merchant of Venice*: A Reconsideration' in '*The Merchant of Venice*': A Selection of Critical Essays, ed. John Wilders, Macmillan, 1969.
2. See Simon Shepherd, 'Shakespeare's Private Drawer' in *The Shakespeare Myth*, ed. Graham Holderness, Manchester University Press, 1988.

Bibliography

NOTE: All quotations are from the New Penguin edition of *The Merchant of Venice*, ed. W. Moelwyn Merchant, Harmondsworth, 1967.

Texts

Charlton Hinman (ed.), *The Norton Facsimile: The First Folio of Shakespeare*, Paul Hamlyn (London and New York, 1968).

M. M. Mahood (ed.), *The Merchant of Venice* (New Cambridge Shakespeare), Cambridge University Press (Cambridge, 1987).

John Russell Brown (ed.), *The Merchant of Venice* (Arden Shakespeare), Methuen (London, 1955).

Criticism

James C. Bulman, *Shakespeare in Performance: 'The Merchant of Venice'*, Manchester University Press (Manchester, 1989).

Graham Holderness, Nick Potter and John Turner, *Shakespeare: The Play of History*, Macmillan (London, 1987).

Laurence Lerner (ed.), *Shakespeare's Comedies: An Anthology of Modern Criticism*, Penguin (Harmondsworth, 1967).

Graham Midgely, '*The Merchant of Venice*: A Reconsideration' from *Essays in Criticism*, (1960) X.

E. M. W. Tillyard, *Shakespeare's Problem Plays*, Chatto and Windus (London, 1950).

John Wilders (ed.), *'The Merchant of Venice': A Selection of Critical Essays*, Macmillan (London, 1969).

Theory

Peter Brook, *The Empty Space*, Penguin (Harmondsworth, 1972), pp. 96–7.

Walter Cohen, '*The Merchant of Venice* and the Possibilities of Historical Criticism', *ELH*, (1982), XLIX:iv.

Stephen Greenblatt, *Shakespearean Negotiations*, Oxford University Press (Oxford, 1988).

Stephen Greenblatt, *Learning to Curse*, Routledge (London, 1990).
Graham Holderness (ed.), *The Shakespeare Myth*, Manchester University Press (Manchester, 1988).

READ MORE IN PENGUIN

In every corner of the world, on every subject under the sun, Penguin represents quality and variety – the very best in publishing today.

For complete information about books available from Penguin – including Puffins, Penguin Classics and Arkana – and how to order them, write to us at the appropriate address below. Please note that for copyright reasons the selection of books varies from country to country.

In the United Kingdom: Please write to *Dept. EP, Penguin Books Ltd, Bath Road, Harmondsworth, West Drayton, Middlesex UB7 ODA*

In the United States: Please write to *Consumer Sales, Penguin USA, P.O. Box 999, Dept. 17109, Bergenfield, New Jersey 07621-0120*. VISA and MasterCard holders call 1-800-253-6476 to order Penguin titles

In Canada: Please write to *Penguin Books Canada Ltd, 10 Alcorn Avenue, Suite 300, Toronto, Ontario M4V 3B2*

In Australia: Please write to *Penguin Books Australia Ltd, P.O. Box 257, Ringwood, Victoria 3134*

In New Zealand: Please write to *Penguin Books (NZ) Ltd, Private Bag 102902, North Shore Mail Centre, Auckland 10*

In India: Please write to *Penguin Books India Pvt Ltd, 706 Eros Apartments, 56 Nehru Place, New Delhi 110 019*

In the Netherlands: Please write to *Penguin Books Netherlands bv, Postbus 3507, NL-1001 AH Amsterdam*

In Germany: Please write to *Penguin Books Deutschland GmbH, Metzlerstrasse 26, 60594 Frankfurt am Main*

In Spain: Please write to *Penguin Books S. A., Bravo Murillo 19, 1° B, 28015 Madrid*

In Italy: Please write to *Penguin Italia s.r.l., Via Felice Casati 20, I–20124 Milano*

In France: Please write to *Penguin France S. A., 17 rue Lejeune, F–31000 Toulouse*

In Japan: Please write to *Penguin Books Japan, Ishikiribashi Building, 2–5–4, Suido, Bunkyo-ku, Tokyo 112*

In South Africa: Please write to *Longman Penguin Southern Africa (Pty) Ltd, Private Bag X08, Bertsham 2013*

READ MORE IN PENGUIN

CRITICAL STUDIES

Described by *The Times Educational Supplement* as 'admirable' and 'superb', Penguin Critical Studies is a specially developed series of critical essays on the major works of literature for use by students in universities, colleges and schools.

Titles published or in preparation include:

William Blake
The Changeling
Doctor Faustus
Emma and Persuasion
Great Expectations
The Great Gatsby
Heart of Darkness
The Poetry of Gerard
  Manley Hopkins
Joseph Andrews
Mansfield Park
Middlemarch
The Mill on the Floss
Paradise Lost
The Poetry of Alexander
  Pope

The Portrait of a Lady
A Portrait of the Artist as a
  Young Man
The Return of the Native
Rosencrantz and Guildenstern
  are Dead
Sons and Lovers
Tennyson
Tess of the D'Urbervilles
To the Lighthouse
The Waste Land
Wordsworth
Wuthering Heights
Yeats

READ MORE IN PENGUIN

CRITICAL STUDIES

Described by *The Times Educational Supplement* as 'admirable' and 'superb', Penguin Critical Studies is a specially developed series of critical essays on the major works of literature for use by students in universities, colleges and schools.

Titles published or in preparation include:

SHAKESPEARE

Antony and Cleopatra
As You Like It
Hamlet
Julius Caesar
King Lear
A Midsummer Night's Dream
Much Ado About Nothing
Othello
Richard II
Romeo and Juliet
Shakespeare – Text into Performance
Shakespeare's History Plays
The Tempest
Troilus and Cressida
The Winter's Tale

CHAUCER

Chaucer
The Pardoner's Tale
The Prologue to the
  Canterbury Tales

READ MORE IN PENGUIN

THE NEW PENGUIN SHAKESPEARE

READ MORE IN PENGUIN

RUDYARD KIPLING

'The most complete man of genius I have ever known' – Henry James

The Light That Failed	The Jungle Books
A Diversity of Creatures	Life's Handicap
The Day's Work	Limits and Renewals
Debits and Credits	Something of Myself
Wee Willie Winkie	Plain Tales from the Hills
Just So Stories	Puck of Pook's Hill
Traffics and Discoveries	Rewards and Fairies
Kim	Stalky and Co.

'For my own part I worshipped Kipling at thirteen, loathed him at seventeen, enjoyed him at twenty, despised him at twenty-five, and now again rather admire him. The one thing that was never possible, if one had read him at all, was to forget him' – George Orwell

READ MORE IN PENGUIN

D. H. LAWRENCE

D. H. Lawrence is acknowledged as one of the greatest writers of the twentieth century. Nearly all his works have been published in Penguin.

NOVELS

Aaron's Rod
The Lost Girl
The Rainbow
The Trespasser
Women in Love
The First Lady Chatterley
The Boy in the Bush

Lady Chatterley's Lover
The Plumed Serpent
Sons and Lovers
The White Peacock
Kangaroo
John Thomas and Lady Jane

SHORT STORIES

Three Novellas: The Fox/
 The Ladybird/The Captain's
 Doll
St Mawr *and* The Virgin and
 the Gipsy
Selected Short Stories

The Prussian Officer
Love Among the Haystacks
The Princess
England, My England
The Woman Who Rode
 Away
The Mortal Coil

TRAVEL BOOKS AND OTHER WORKS

Mornings in Mexico
Studies in Classic
 American Literature
Apocalypse

Fantasia of the Unconscious
 and Psychoanalysis and the
 Unconscious
D. H. Lawrence and Italy

POETRY

D. H. Lawrence: Selected Poetry
Edited and Introduced by Keith Sagar

PLAYS

Three Plays

READ MORE IN PENGUIN

CHARLES DICKENS

'A popular and fecund, but yet profound, serious and wonderfully resourceful practising novelist, a master of it' – Q. D. Leavis

'He was successful beyond any English novelist, probably beyond any novelist that has ever lived, in exactly hitting off the precise tone of thought and feeling' – Leslie Stephen

'All the political futility which has forced men of the calibre of Mussolini, Kemal and Hitler to assume dictatorship might have been saved if people had only believed what Dickens told them in *Little Dorrit*' – Bernard Shaw

'Heaven for the just: for the wicked, Hell. Herein Dickens is true to the opinion of his countrymen and of his time' – André Gide

'Language and morality add dimensions to his cartoons and turn them into literature' – Anthony Burgess

Barnaby Rudge
The Christmas Books
Dombey and Son
Hard Times
Martin Chuzzlewit
Nicholas Nickleby
Oliver Twist
The Pickwick Papers
American Notes for General
   Circulation

Bleak House
David Copperfield
Great Expectations
Little Dorrit
The Mystery of Edwin
   Drood
The Old Curiosity Shop
Out Mutual Friend
A Tale of Two Cities
Selected Short Fiction

READ MORE IN PENGUIN

THOMAS HARDY

'Hardy is one of the relatively few writers who produced, by common consent, both major fiction and major poetry' – Martin Seymour-Smith

Tess of the D'Urbervilles
'An extraordinarily beautiful book ... Perhaps this is another way of saying that *Tess* is a poetic novel' – A. Alvarez

Far From the Madding Crowd
'The novel which announced Hardy's arrival as a great writer' – Ronald Blythe

A Pair of Blue Eyes
'Hardy's first significantly autobiographical work to achieve publication, and the first to bear the author's name' – Roger Ebbatson

Jude the Obscure
'The characters ... are built up not merely against the background of the huge and now changing Wessex, but out of it. It is this which makes the novel the completion of an oeuvre' – C. H. Sisson

The Woodlanders
'In no other novel does Hardy seem more confidently in control of what he has to say, more assured of the tone in which to say it' – Ian Gregor

The Return of the Native
'It came to embody more faithfully than any other book the quintessence of all that Wessex already represented in Hardy's mind' – George Woodcock

The Mayor of Casterbridge
In depicting a man who overreaches the limits, Hardy once again demonstrates his uncanny psychological grasp and his deeply rooted knowledge of mid-nineteenth century Dorset.

and
The Trumpet-Major
Under the Greenwood Tree
The Distracted Preacher and Other Tales

READ MORE IN PENGUIN

THE PLAYS OF BERNARD SHAW

'Shaw has redeemed and embellished our fantasies' – Raymond Williams. The complete dramatic works of Bernard Shaw are now published in paperback for the first time, definitive texts under the editorial supervision of Dan H. Laurence.

THE BERNARD SHAW LIBRARY

Androcles and the Lion
The Apple Cart
Back to Methuselah
The Doctor's Dilemma
Getting Married/Press Cuttings
Heartbreak House
Major Barbara
Man and Superman
Plays Extravagant
(The Millionairess, Too True to be Good, The Simpleton of the Unexpected Isles)
Plays Pleasant
(Arms and the Man, Candida, The Man of Destiny, You Never Can Tell)
Plays Political
(The Apple Cart, On the Rocks, Geneva)
Plays Unpleasant
(Widowers' Houses, The Philanderer, Mrs Warren's Profession)
Pygmalion
Saint Joan
Selected Short Plays
(including The Admirable Bashville and Great Catherine)
The Shewing-Up of Blanco Posnet and **Fanny's First Play**
Three Plays for Puritans
(The Devil's Disciple, Caesar and Cleopatra, Captain Brassbound's Conversion)

PUBLISHED IN PENGUIN PLAYS

John Bull's Other Island
Misalliance and the Fascinating Foundling

READ MORE IN PENGUIN

A SELECTION OF PLAYS

Edward Albee	Who's Afraid of Virginia Woolf?
Alan Ayckbourn	Joking Apart and Other Plays
Dermot Bolger	A Dublin Quartet
Bertolt Brecht	Parables for the Theatre
Anton Chekhov	Plays (The Cherry Orchard/Three Sisters/ Ivanov//The Seagull/Uncle Vania)
Henrik Ibsen	A Doll's House/League of Youth/Lady from the Sea
Eugène Ionesco	Rhinoceros/The Chairs/The Lesson
Ben Jonson	Three Comedies (Volpone/The Alchemist/ Bartholomew Fair)
D. H. Lawrence	Three Plays (The Collier's Friday Night/ The Daughter-in-Law/The Widowing of Mrs Holroyd)
Arthur Miller	Death of a Salesman
John Mortimer	A Voyage Round My Father/What Shall We Tell Caroline?/The Dock Brief
J. B. Priestley	Time and the Conways/I Have Been Here Before/An Inspector/The Linden Tree
Peter Shaffer	Lettice and Lovage/Yonadab
Bernard Shaw	Plays Pleasant (Arms and the Man/ Candida /The Man of Destiny/You Never Can Tell)
Sophocles	Three Theban Plays (Oedipus the King/ Antigone/ Oedipus at Colonus)
Wendy Wasserstein	The Heidi Chronicles and Other Plays
Keith Waterhouse	Jeffrey Bernard is Unwell and Other Plays
Arnold Wesker	Plays, Volume 1: The Wesker Trilogy (Chicken Soup with Barley/Roots/I'm Talking about Jerusalem)
Oscar Wilde	The Importance of Being Earnest and Other Plays
Thornton Wilder	Our Town/The Skin of Our Teeth/The Matchmaker
Tennessee Williams	Cat on a Hot Tin Roof/The Milk Train Doesn't Stop Here Anymore/The Night of the Iguana